Face to Face with Terror

From the Vienna OPEC Attack
to the Terrorism of Today
by Ingrid Weiss

Ingrid Weiss

Face to Face with Terror

From the Vienna OPEC Attack to the Terrorism of Today

A factual report

Translated by
Marlene Krammer-Campbell

Ibera

European University Press

The current volume was first published in German in November 2004 with the title "Der sich dem Terror stellte". Thus, the English translation is identical to the original German version with the exception of Chapter 19, which has been newly updated by Dr. Rawenduzy.

© 2004 - First German edition
Ingrid Weiss
Der sich dem Terror stellte
Vom Wiener Opec Überfall zum Terrorismus der Gegenwart
ISBN 3-85052-220-2

Die Deutsche Bibliothek – CIP-Einheitsaufnahme
Weiss, Ingrid:
Face to face with terror / Ingrid Weiss. – Vienna:
European University Press / Ibera Verlag, 2006
ISBN 3-85052-219-9

Editor translation: Jeffrey Ulrich
Printing and bound by Ebner & Spiegel, Ulm, Germany, EU

ISBN 3-85052-219-9

www. ibera.at

Contents

What Would You Like to Know, My Dear?

Christmas, 2002

Peter I. Tschaikovsky's Piano Concerto in B-Minor presses upon my mind. The pearly, effervescent tones coil upon each other and into me, and I feel I must reconsider my request, must think through it critically. What would I like to know, really?

Many things I already know.

The man in question is an Austrian. And he is an Iraqi, Kurdistan-born.

He is a doctor. In addition, he is a doctor of Internal Medicine and a true credit to his profession, a man who helps anywhere and everywhere he can.

He is my friend. Moreover, the basis of our friendship is trust and intellectual interchange.

And to top it off, he is a living giant of contemporary history.

He is Doctor Wiriya Rawenduzy.

I met Dr. Rawenduzy more than ten years ago while I was working for the Austrian Red Cross and he was heading the doctor's team at the Red Cross Blood Bank. He was polite and dedicated to his work, and never spoke about himself, or about what was on his mind. Above all he never spoke about what he had done for Austria, what he had done out of a mere promise, done so matter-of-factly, so gratefully even, what he had done at a time when "Operation Terror" had been a mere word, a vague picture in the imagination, but still a word without any true meaning for Austrians.

During my tenure at the Red Cross, chronic lower back pain forced me to seek the help of the Red Cross staff doctor of Internal Medicine, who I soon learned to be Dr. Wiriya Rawenduzy. His office was only a flight of stairs up from mine, which made it relatively easy to obtain relief when I was in pain.

There, in Dr. Rawenduzy's office, between the taking of blood pressure, the use of the stethoscope, and the giving of injections, Dr. Rawenduzy and I came to share short philosophical discussions on basic principles of life. Although we worked in different departments of the Red Cross we were both aware that basic life principles were the centerpiece of any life well-lived. Yet despite our conversations, I had trouble understanding who this friendly, yet serious-looking physician really was.

Eventually two of my co-workers, both of whom had been at the Austrian Red Cross much longer than I, and hence had become familiar with the private lives of the employees, cleared it up for me. He was the doctor of The Terrorist. He had been, and still was, world-famous.

But had I not known, queried my co-workers, flabbergasted, who it was that had contributed, through his spontaneous action and self-sacrificing courage, to these recent and important events here in Austria? The women looked at me reproachfully. Had I never heard the name "Carlos", they wondered aloud. Or perhaps mention of an attack on "OPEC" might ring a bell for me.

Yes, I did remember. A hold-up at OPEC around Christmas. Hostages. Bloodshed. Chancellor Kreisky and an Austrian Airlines plane. All of these images flashed through my mind.

Yes, of course I remembered those days. They had left us Austrians numb with shock as we headed into the Christmas season. But why were these things relevant now, and how on earth could they be connected to Dr. Rawenduzy, this simple physician of the Austrian Red Cross Blood Bank?

I became curious. Perhaps I should ask him about it the next time we met accidentally in the hallway or dining room. Why had he never mentioned anything about it in our conversations? Did he not wish to talk about it?

I had already learned that he was a Kurd, so I tried to refresh my memory of Middle East history. Kurds. Iraq. The Shah of Persia ... Oil and unbearable human suffering. But despite such a tumultuous history, what could the attack on OPEC possibly have to do with a Kurdish doctor working for the Austrian Red Cross?

I did not see the connection. Each time I had the chance to address the matter to Dr. Rawenduzy personally (my lumbar pain reoccurred regularly), my courage seemed to fail me.

I could not put the pieces together without help, but what right did I have to ask him for information? Could I justify asking by virtue of the fact that we both worked for the Red Cross and needed to know and trust each other in order to work together? Could I ask him while he was on duty? An emphatic no. What then? To play it off as female curiosity, even in the positive sense of the word, did not seem proper given my position as Secretary-General. To cautiously interview my co-workers was equally inconceivable. It would only create chit-chat and gossip. So how to approach this man?

In the end, the question was resolved by my busy schedule. My duties at the Austrian Red Cross left me little time or opportunity to dwell extensively on the subject. My job was strenuous and consumed nearly twenty-four hours a day, and in addition, my husband and I were raising a young daughter who demanded my undivided attention every evening, even when I returned home drained and exhausted. Moreover, for some reason I had the feeling that my 'personal' physician, as I had secretly come to think of Dr. Rawenduzy, had no desire to discuss the matter with me.

I accepted this.

Some years passed. I voluntarily resigned my position as Secretary-General and left the Austrian Red Cross. I made this decision because I could not rectify certain conflicting views within the organization with my convictions. Furthermore, my daughter had reached school age and I could not sacrifice her well-being to further my career. I had always longed for a child, and above all, my family was far too important to me.

I remained in contact with Dr. Rawenduzy. I trusted him and drove regularly across Vienna to his office in Donaustadt. Time passed, but he did not change. He remained friendly, polite, and ready to help.

Still I hesitated to inquire about the terrorist attack. I did not truly forget it; I merely pushed it to the back of my mind. And often when Dr. Rawenduzy looked at me through his gold-rimmed glasses, I thought I detected a message in his gaze: Patients are patients, and they are not entitled to ask questions outside the medical field.

Again, I accepted what I perceived to be the Doctor's wishes. More years passed.

I remained Dr. Rawenduzy's patient until his well-deserved retirement, after which he closed his office. His son followed in his footsteps and opened an office in Donaustadt, and soon Dr. Rawenduzy and I lost contact. When I thought about it, it hardly seemed possible that he was no longer in my life. I had grown used to my 'personal' physician. Who would be there to answer my medical questions? I had reached a point in life where I looked at other people, especially unknown doctors, with an exceedingly critical eye. One's own body, one's health, is a great treasure, and I did not want to consign mine to just any old doctor.

Several months passed. My health was stable and I ignored the inner voice that told me I should search for another doctor. I did not want to have the same experience as one of my girlfriends, also a patient of Dr. Rawenduzy, who had met with her new doctor for five minutes without his once looking her in the eye or, apparently, realizing she was a human being. Five minutes, and then he had been through with her. Next patient, please!

Soon fall had arrived. School was in full swing. My life had fallen into a structured routine. Rise early, teach, take care of family and household, prepare for classes, and then grade mountains of English compositions. I rarely had time to devote to my great love, philosophy. My free time was restricted to reading the newspaper. Personally, I did not see a way to escape the pressure of the many things I had to do, so I gave in to the routine. Did I give in consciously? No. Probably unconsciously.

Then suddenly the daily rhythm was interrupted by a fax from Dr. Rawenduzy. I could not believe it. What in the world had prompted my 'personal' physician to contact me? Me, of all people.

Perhaps there was a philosophical, principles-of-life problem to be dealt with. But why would he want to discuss such a thing with me? No, it could not be that.

Hurriedly I took the sheet from the fax machine, careful not to tear it. I held my breath and read the short message quickly.

Dear Dr. Weiss,

Kindly call me. Having returned from Kurdistan I would like to see a project become reality (the construction of an orphanage). Financing seems secured. Would like to discuss the entire project with you.

Best Regards,

Dr. W. Rawenduzy

With mixed feelings, I put the message aside, only to pick it up a few minutes later. Why me? My work at the Austrian Red Cross had ended long ago; Dr. Rawenduzy knew that. My job as a teacher at a Viennese School was not at all relevant to the matter. Strange. Yet in spite of my uncertainty, I was curious.

His request sounded urgent, so I wished to respond quickly. Would it be best to call Dr. Rawenduzy, or should I answer by fax? I was convinced my 'personal' physician expected a quick reply, so I picked up the telephone, only to realize that I had no number. The phone book would help. However, I was out of luck; there was no listing. For my second attempt, I called directory assistance. A gruff, female voice at the other end of the line informed me that the number I was looking for did indeed exist, but unfortunately was unlisted. I begged, in vain. Rules were rules. Outraged, I slammed down the receiver. How could I get in touch with Dr. Rawenduzy without either a telephone number or a private address? Ah, I spied a glimmer of hope, a solution. The sender of the fax! Why had I not thought of it before? I smiled at my shortcomings. Typical. I picked up the fax, relieved.

But alas, there was no number from the sender. Rage and despair took hold of me. What should I do?

"Just don't answer it," I said aloud. Yes, that was the solution. Offended by life and disappointed I went into the next room. My piano.

I had an insatiable urge to play. As a child, I had played the piano to restore my inner peace. Today Chopin seemed suitable. My fingers flew over the keys and I practically felt the music tickle my skin. Yes.

You once received a business card from Dr. Rawenduzy. In the middle of my piano session, the words flashed through my mind. I jumped up, Chopin forgotten. What had I done with his business card? Damn it. My handbag is always such a mess. Years ago, my friend Inge had given me a special business card organizer, but I had never used it. Wallet, mirror, keys, lipstick, handkerchiefs ... many pens (predominantly red ones, important for teachers), hair brush, some crumpled notes ... but no business card. Where on earth is this piece of paper? Perhaps in my calendar. I often file things in my calendar. A bad habit, I know. I had come to call my calendar my second brain. Nervously I rooted through the scraps of paper that had accumulated there since the beginning of the year.

Yes! Overjoyed I leapt into the air and let out a cry of glee. The door into the room was flung open and I felt the questioning glance of Mirela, my daughter.

"I've found it! I've found it!" I cried. Of course, my tone scarcely resembled that of Britney Spears, so Mirela turned around, shaking her head. Without a word she hurried back to her room, and seconds later the deafening tones of "I'm a Girl, Not Yet a Woman!" vibrated through the apartment. How right Ms. Spears was.

Dr. W. Rawenduzy, M.D. Specialist of Internal Medicine

I could not believe my eyes. There on the card was the telephone number of the doctor's office, but it had been closed for some time. Was today Friday the thirteenth? Had I gotten up on the wrong side of the bed? What was the matter with the world today? Normally I am not superstitious, but such a string of bad luck was simply not possible. Moreover, Knopfi, our four-legged domestic companion, was a dog, not a black cat.

I took a deep breath. Ponder. I noticed vaguely that I was rotating the calling card in my nervous hands. Then still lost in thought I observed that I was dialing the number. Perhaps there was an answering service. I hoped so.

"Dr. Rawenduzy's office," a voice chimed through the receiver.

I was startled. Who? What?!?

I stammered my name and the friendly female voice at the other end greeted me cordially. She had not heard from me in quite some time. It came to me in a flash. Of course. That was Mrs. Schneider, the former assistant to my 'personal' physician. Slowly, I understood. The older son of Dr. Rawenduzy had not taken over his father's office at all—only the telephone number. Mrs. Schneider had decided to join Dr. Rawenduzy Jr. We chatted for a few minutes, and finally Mrs. Schneider gave me the private address and telephone number of her former boss. Done.

There in my apartment, my coffee machine looked at me with a silvery smile. I treated myself to a small espresso topped with foamed milk, my favorite drink if coffee discussions are relevant. Meanwhile Britney Spears had finished her performance through the wall of my daughter's room, the question of whether she was now a girl or a woman remaining open. Our dog stretched comfortably in his sleep. She had never had a problem with any of this.

A sonorous voice answered the phone after the second ring.

"Rawenduzy."

He was glad I had responded so quickly. If only he knew how I had suffered. However, the issue of the orphanage was far too complex to discuss over the phone. He was familiar with much of my history and knew I was greatly experienced in these matters. Furthermore, he was convinced I would gladly share my expertise. After all, the project concerned children. Countless, unimaginably poor children. Orphans.

Immediately I agreed to get involved. We made an appointment for an afternoon the following week, in one of those cozy cafés in downtown Vienna where one could relax while feasting the palate on a sweet treat. I have been enraptured with Vienna since birth and have ever had a deep love for and loyalty to the peaceful city's coffee houses. Perfect.

The next days passed quickly. The afternoon drew nearer, and with it our meeting in said café. When the day arrived, I took the subway into the city center. Driving left an open door to too many potential problems. I could get stuck in traffic, or spend hours finding a parking place. Parking in Vienna was always a thing of mere chance anyway, and I wanted to avoid being late.

Downtown I looked nervously at a clock on the street as I hurried along the Graben, one of Vienna's most famous boulevards. Still a few minutes left. I slowed my pace. I did not want to be too early. Beautifully decorated and marvelously equipped storefronts caught my eye, but only for a fleeting moment. After all, I was deeply in thought over the upcoming meeting. I arrived at the café, and as I opened the door to enter, my body tensed.

I looked from table to table. Had he not arrived yet? Was I indeed too early? I took off one of my gloves and glanced at my watch.

"Hello," said a familiar voice. "I am glad you could come."

I was relieved. Dr. Rawenduzy took me to a cozy corner close to the window, where we sat at a small table with two chairs. We chatted about the weather, about our children, about work, and about the old days at the Austrian Red Cross. I enjoyed my espresso with foamed milk, and treated myself to a piece of sweet chestnut cake. Dr. Rawenduzy had just a mélange (a black coffee with milk) and a glass of water. Friendly. Polite. And not equipped with a stethoscope.

I examined my personal physician. It was the first time I had ever met him privately. The short, white, curly hair encircling his skin, the bold face, and the black roll-neck collar sweater underscored his masculine features. He gazed steadily at me. Would I be willing to share my international experience with street children and orphanages with the project he had mentioned in the fax? The project was planned for the Iraqi part of Kurdistan.

I felt my gray cells fired up. My social conscience reacted, and immediately I agreed. He gave me a detailed description of the children's living conditions and provided me with photos. He had personally taken these photos several weeks ago in Iraq. They touched me deeply, and looking at them, I found it difficult to breath. They made me think of my daughter.

We arranged another meeting, and I promised to prepare a precise list of all pedagogical and psychological principles which seemed relevant to the success of the project.

Some months passed.

We met on a regular basis. I tried to keep my promise and made the list as comprehensive as possible. I went over it again and again, boring into the details and adding personal experiences and relevant scientific data. I hoped to make a small contribution to the project.

Spring had arrived. The sun beamed warmth down on Vienna. Coffee houses on the Graben and in the surrounding alleys had opened their outdoor gardens. We took pleasure in continuing our conversations outdoors over coffee with apple strudel or cake. Dr. Rawenduzy was preparing for his next trip to Iraqi Kurdistan, and he wanted me to be there when the foundation for the orphanage was laid. On the same trip, he intended to hold lectures for the medical students at the University of Sulaymania.

By this time, our conversations had ceased to focus exclusively on the orphanage, and I had tried several times to lead our discussions carefully toward the past. I had not forgotten the issue that had implanted itself into my brain that day with my two coworkers at the Austrian Red Cross. This man was the doctor of "The Terrorist". I hinted, and I pried, and I assumed my hints and my prying were subtle and undetectable until one day, in an action typical of him, he unmasked me with a simple, direct question.

"What, my dear Dr. Weiss, would you liked to know?" he asked.

I almost stopped breathing. Had I gone too far? How should I now formulate a reply? It was embarrassing, and I was blushing. My now-teenage daughter would have told me to 'keep it cool', but I was not succeeding in keeping it cool.

Ill at ease and feeling backed into a corner I decided, obstinately, on a counterattack.

"At Red Cross headquarters I was told that you had been a doctor of a terrorist. The name Carlos was mentioned. What connections did you have to this person, to this… international terrorist?"

Now it was out in the open. My voice had not faltered but under the coffee table, my knees were trembling.

Uncertainly I began to stir the milky foam into my espresso. For long seconds there was a deafening silence at our table. The laughter and chit-chat of the people in the café seemed to have enclosed us. Then, almost imperceptibly, he bent forward and put his hand on my arm.

"That is part of the story of my life," he said smiling. "If I told you everything you could write a book about it."

Wiriya Rawenduzy's father Muhammed Amin Rawenduzy,
and mother Nadjia Fatah. Rawenduz, 1952

The Beginning of the Struggle for Survival

The sun shone mercilessly on the boys as they played. It was a hot day in July, and Baghdad seemed to be boiling. The eight-year-old Wiriya and his friends, however, were immersed in their games. Their marbles bounced on the ground and, tricky as they were, disappeared into small holes in the sand. The boys loved these glass beads. They cared for them like treasures and stored them carefully in small brown leather bags.

Suddenly Wiriya leapt to his feet. Ali looked at him quizzically. Did he not wish to continue playing?

Ibrahim, another of the boys, ran his hand uncertainly through his hair, then pushed Wiriya impatiently back toward the beads.

"Come on. You're next. Play," he said.

But Wiriya had already collected his marbles and put them back into the small bag. Ali, Wiriya's best friend, became angry. Why did Wiriya have to go now?

Wiriya half-turned. It was mealtime in his family, he explained. He was already very late and he had to hurry. Father hated any kind of tardiness.

Little Wiriya was the eldest child of his family, so he knew his duties. Punctuality was one of them, and he was late. For this reason, in his heart of hearts, the boy was hoping that his father would be absent from lunch. This was often the case. Wiriya's father, Muhammed Amin Rawenduzy, was the highest-ranking officer of a garrison of the Iraqi military, and his duties frequently kept him away from his children and his beloved wife Nadija for extended periods.

Returning home, Wiriya opened the door breathlessly and flung his small leather bag into a corner. The dining room door was open, but inside the table was empty. The clock on the wall, normally kind to the boy, pointed its menacing hands at him. Wiriya was half an hour late.

What should he do? The whole house was quiet. Perhaps they had all gone out. On the table, the boy spied a plate covered with a linen napkin. His stomach was rumbling. Apparently, his mother had left food for him and had covered it with a linen napkin to protect it from flies.

What was on the menu today, Wiriya wondered? He loved it when his mother made Dolma. Hopefully it was Dolma, and hopefully this time she had stuffed it with more than just rice. Dolma was stuffed eggplant and it tasted best filled with a bit of chopped meat. The boy pulled the chair away from the table and sat down. He was alone in the room, but alone or not, he was used to keeping strict table manners. His posture at the table was to be upright, and he did not lean back on the chair. The back was to be straight, and one lifted the fork to the mouth without excessively bending over the plate. The napkin should stay on the lap, and (father insisted on this point especially) there was to be absolutely no smacking of the lips, regardless of how hungry one was.

Wiriya was proud of his father and wanted his father to be proud of him. Carefully, with a ritual-like solemnity, he removed the linen napkin from the plate and placed it over his small lap. He picked up his knife and fork and...

What was this? He froze. Tears began to run down his small cheeks. Under the napkin on the plate instead of his beloved Dolma, there stared up at him a big, gray rock.

Instantly Wiriya understood. He had not fulfilled his duty of being on time, so he was not entitled to food.

Many years passed. Father had again been transferred and the family had moved from Baghdad to Erbil, a town in Iraqi Kurdistan. The political situation was tense. King Gazi had recently been killed in a car accident, and his son was still a child. His uncle had temporarily taken over the regency, but had fled when the Pro-British government was replaced by a coup. Now the members of the royal family feared for their lives. Desperate, the Queen and her young son Faisal had taken refuge in Erbil, where she had begged on her knees for the help of the military commander of Erbil, Muhammed Amin Rawenduzy, pleading for him to grant her and her family asylum.

Everyone knew that Muhammed Amin Rawenduzy was a man of honor. He was a Kurd, and a very politically-active individual, and he always stood up for the rights of the people no matter what it meant for himself. He despised corruption in any form, and he fought it with all means at his disposal. It was well known that anyone who asked him for protection would have it.

Muhammed Amin Rawenduzy put a house in a suburb of Erbil at the disposal of the Queen and her son, with fifty soldiers to stand guard day and night. The order was clear: anyone who even came close to the building was to be shot immediately, and Commander Rawenduzy personally made sure that this order was strictly obeyed.

One day, when Wiriya was twelve years old, he was permitted to accompany his father to the Queen's temporary home. They arrived at her place of exile and the boy exchanged some words with the Queen and then spoke with the Queen's son Faisal, who was slightly younger than Wiriya.

"A king must have a kingdom," Wiriya said to the boy. "Where is yours?"

Faisal did not fully understand the question; he was too young. However, before the young Prince could respond, Muhammed Amin Rawenduzy raised his hand and, in front of everyone, gave Wiriya a hard slap in the face.

Again, like the day at the dinner table before the napkin-covered rock, the boy understood instantly. Just as punctuality was one of his absolutely duties, so was politeness.

In the following years, Wiriya concentrated not only on school but also on sports. The family moved again. Father became the military commander of Hilla, a town in Central Iraq. Wiriya was an enthusiastic soccer player and had once scored the decisive goal in a school tournament. In his school he was treated as a hero, even more than your normal high school star athlete, because his school had not just won the much-coveted local golden trophy but had also been named the Soccer Champions of Central Iraq.

As a result, soon Wiriya was granted many special privileges. For example, in the afternoon, while other students were required to take classes in English or religion, Wiriya was allowed to practice soccer. Success in sports was preferred to success in academics.

Wiriya's mother, a teacher by trade, who had given up her profession after getting married, had mixed feelings about Wiriya's increasing emphasis on athletics. Besides watching over her son's education, her special hobby had become holistic medicine. She was familiar with all the plants and herbs growing in Iraq. She prepared concoctions and tried to ease people's pains or even heal their diseases. In those days in Central Iraq, medical care as it exists in Central Europe today was unheard of.

Muhammed Amin Rawenduzy took great pains to insure a comprehensive education for his son. Of course, he was proud that Wiriya was such an excellent athlete, but at the same time Commander Rawenduzy demanded outstanding grades. For example, in the six weeks prior to the final exams for high school, young Wiriya had to study up to twelve hours a day. His only food during this time was fruit, bread, and water. More than five thousand students in Central Iraq had registered for that final test; only four received top marks in every subject, and Wiriya was one of them. Strict discipline was not just a mere slogan in the Rawenduzy household. It was a living reality.

Because of his superior achievement, it was only logical for Wiriya to be sent to university. However, since his family was Kurdish the odds that he would be accepted at the University of Baghdad's Medical School, were extremely slim.

In Iraq, the Kurds were not a free people. They had long been suppressed by all Iraqi governments, had been stripped of their civil rights, and had been treated as second-class citizens. The Kurds, as a people, are one of the oldest civilized nations in the world; yet arbitrary acts of injustice had been and still were a daily event in Iraq, without any reprisal in sight (A fact that has even intensified in present times, interestingly enough). As the powers that be in the rest of the world looked on, the tireless struggle for autonomy of this brave people continued then and continues to this day.

Despite the family's Kurdish heritage, Muhammed Amin Rawenduzy was a highly respected man, and through his contacts he managed to obtain for his son admission to the University of Baghdad, a privilege normally reserved for the upper crust of Iraqi society.

For the first two semesters of his university career, the young student passed all of his examinations with high marks. Next to his studies, he became more and more involved in politics. He felt his Kurdish origin in each fiber of his athletic body, and knew it was his duty to stand up for his people. Soon his enthusiasm had fused with his extraordinary intelligence to make him one of the most important minds in the Kurdish liberation movement. Among other things, he organized demonstrations, which the police met with extreme force. Soon political activities became more and more dangerous, and consequently more and more underground.

Wiriya's third semester began without incident. Wiriya had performed extraordinarily in his first year of studies, so he expected to pass the third semester easily. In fact, according the Iraqi University regulations and his prior record, it was technically impossible for him to fail in his third semester. In

Wiriya's mind, this was ideal; it made it easier to devote his attention to politics.

Then a summons to appear before the dean of the university changed the course of his life forever. The dean informed Wiriya Rawenduzy that the young student's political activities had become incongruous with his studies at the Medical School. It had been decided that he was henceforth barred from any further medical studies, and was forbidden to even set foot on university property. In addition, he was exceedingly fortunate not to have landed in jail.

No one remembered that it was Wiriya Rawenduzy who had won the silver medal in the high jump of the University Games. The king himself had placed the medal around his neck.

Distraught, the young man cleared his tiny rented room in Baghdad and went home to Erbil, where his parents and siblings lived in a row house. His father was now retired.

Determined to persevere, Wiriya continued on his political path. Within a few months, he had become the head of the illegal Kurdish Liberation Organization, where he was responsible for Erbil and the surrounding provinces.

The police responded. By this time Wiriya Rawenduzy was under constant police surveillance, but cautiously and even more persistently he continued his work underground. August 1949 approached. Suddenly he received news that one of his followers had been arrested. It was clear that he had to leave Erbil at once.

Frenzied, he hurried to a car that was to take him to Kirkuk. But it was too late. Handcuffs were slapped onto his wrists and Wiriya Rawenduzy was taken to the Erbil prison like a common criminal. From there he was transferred to Schaklawe, where the head of the Iraqi Secret Service awaited him. Wiriya learned that the police had amassed devastating evidence against him, including decoded messages from himself to several of his 300 activists.

There in the Secret Service Office in Schaklawe, Wiriya, the Kurd, looked at his captors, read the cynical smile of the Secret Service Agent before him, and knew that his situation was bad. If he did not confess, he would be tortured brutally. He saw no way out, so he confessed and took full responsibility for all of the crimes implicated by the evidence. Rawenduzy was sentenced to solitary confinement in the prison of Abu-Ghraib, under the most terrible of conditions.

The cell measured two meters in length by one and a half meter in width. There was no light. There was little water. There were tiny portions of inadequate, mostly rotten food. And there was psychological terror. Wiriya lived under constant threat of execution. He was permitted to visit the toilet only once a day.

Wiriya endured these tortures for three months, never betraying any of the other activists in his movement. Then a surprising verdict came down from the military court.

Guilty.

However, due to services rendered to Iraq by Muhammed Amin Rawenduzy, Wiriya had been sentenced to only two, rather than twenty years, in prison. After he had served the sentence, he would be released but would remain under constant police surveillance for two more years.

Wiriya knew he had to remain silent, although to do so tore his heart out. His lips tightly pressed together, his dark eyes flooded with hatred, he was taken away.

He was immediately transferred to Baghdad's Central Prison, where he was interred in a barracks built exclusively for political prisoners. There were only three cells, each meant for four to six people. Rawenduzy was put in cell one, which already housed the Secretary-General of the KDP (Kurdish Democratic Party) and three prominent members of opposition parties.

Then, unexpectedly, several days later, Wiriya Rawenduzy was picked up and taken from the prison. He was to be transferred to the prison of Kirkuk. His father had exercised all of the influence at his disposal in order to secure the transfer. Kirkuk was only two hours by car from Erbil, and as a result, the family would be able to visit Wiriya more often.

After only a week, Rawenduzy learned about the corrupt dealings of the warden of the prison. In those days, it was the practice in Iraqi prisons for prisoners with life sentences to serve out their time with heavy chains on their ankles. However, at the Kirkuk prison, if the prisoners paid a prescribed monthly fee to the warden (which was usually saved up at great pains by the prisoners' families), the heavy chains were replaced by lighter ones.

Wiriya could not restrain himself. The entire country was corrupt, but this was clearly going too far. Secretly, Wiriya wrote a report describing the unbearable conditions in the prison. The news reached the office of the editor of a newspaper, illegally of course. The resulting scandal was perfect, and the warden was fired.

However, before long the police discovered who had written the report, and as punishment Wiriya was again transferred. This time it was to a jail in the south of Iraq, in the middle of the desert, in a place called Kut. Certainly, thought the Iraqi authorities, this would break the will of this obnoxious and difficult Kurd.

The conditions in Kut were indescribable. The prisoners were utterly bereft of dignity. The word 'inhuman' would be a kind adjective to describe the horror there. The political prisoners were kept in abominable states of confinement even worse than that of the criminal inmates. Only two things enabled Wiriya to survive this inferno: his unbending pride, and his belief in justice.

A Journey to Somewhere

"He who does not move
will not feel his shackles."
Rosa Luxemburg

The compartment was sparsely occupied, and inside it several travelers were immersed in their newspapers. Others had closed their eyes. It was the Rome-Vienna train, and tonight it was mostly on time, but the slight delay did not really matter. The next stop was Klagenfurt.

The sun had just set, painting the landscape a warm red. The scenery was simply romantic. Lush meadows and deep green lakes nestled snuggly at the foot of proud mountains. The air streamed in through a slightly opened window. It was invigorating.

It was August. More precisely, it was August 11, 1953.

In the compartment, a young main lingered on restless thoughts. He had tremendous confidence in his future, but he still wondered if he would make it here, alone, in a strange country, in a strange city, without any knowledge of the native tongue, which was German.

In a few hours, he would arrive at the train station in Vienna, and no one would be there to meet him. In Vienna, the political situation was tense; Austria was still not free. Even now, years after the end of the Second World War, it was still controlled by the four Allied Forces.

A city controlled by foreign powers. It made Wiriya Rawenduzy shiver and look back on his recent past.

He had hardly been released from the prison in Kut when the police had begun to harass him. He was forbidden to leave Rawenduz, at that time the home of his family, who had moved there before his release. He was not permitted to resume his studies. Several times per day, he had to check in personally with the local police and certify his presence with his signature. It was clear that the authorities resorted to such chicanery simply to wear down this stubborn Kurd.

Wiriya, however, did not give up. He needed to earn money, so he accepted any kind of odd job he could find, from construction worker to substitute teacher, and did each job conscientiously.

Two years passed. He sent applications to the admissions boards of various European universities. He wanted very much to continue his medical studies and was determined to find the right place. He had not buried his dream of becoming a doctor. Finally, he was accepted into the Alma Mater Rudolfina in Vienna, Austria, one of the oldest and most renowned universities in Europe.

He and his family were indescribably happy. Relatives and friends came to say goodbye. Everything had to be done very quickly, for if the Iraqi authorities caught wind of his plans, he would likely be arrested.

A friend of his father donated his entire savings to finance Wiriya's education, and Wiriya packed his suitcases in a hurry. He boarded the bus to Beirut shedding tears of joy. Saying goodbye to his family was extremely painful, and he had to force himself not to wonder if he would ever see them again.

The bus ride from Baghdad to Beirut seemed endless, despite abundant tea breaks and comfortable air conditioning. The border controls took forever. Each suitcase was opened and its contents thoroughly checked.

From Beirut, Wiriya journeyed by boat to Naples. The weather forecast for the coming days cast a pallor over his mood, for it indicated that the passage might become stormy. Indeed, out in the open sea the untamed waves played an interesting game, gushing and roaring and tossing white crowns of foam far up over the railing of the boat. As many sea-voyagers do, Wiriya became sea-sick, vomiting often although he fought it bravely.

Oh how he hated this voyage.

After four days, the worst had passed, and regally, majestically, the huge passenger ship entered the port of Naples by night.

Wiriya needed to find lodging immediately, a task which he thought could prove difficult, for hotel prices were high and the rooms were often deplorably small and dirty, a situation which did not suit Wiriya. Finally, he teamed up with a family from Hamburg he had met on the boat, and together they booked a room. It was not the most relaxing solution, but everyone saved money.

Early in the morning, Wiriya left on the train for Rome. Rome's train station, Roma Termini, was like an anthill. People dashed from platform to platform, only to disappear into trains that looked like giant metal snakes. Wiriya Rawenduzy quickened his step so as not to miss his train to Vienna.

To Vienna. The words were music in his ears. "Vienna, Vienna, here I come," he heard himself intone excitedly. He looked around the compartment, startled to realize he had been singing in a public place. No one had taken any notice of him.

The train left Rome and speeded to Klagenfurt. Then, from Klagenfurt, it was only five hours to the destination of his dreams. Exhausted from the strain of travel, Wiriya fell asleep.

It was past midnight when the direct train from Rome arrived in Vienna. The travelers on the train had already moved their luggage close to the doors so as not to lose any time in exiting. A strange urgency had spread through the train, engulfing Rawenduzy. He kept feeling he must check that he had not forgotten anything.

Suddenly the train jolted. The passengers on their feet stumbled and struggled to remain standing. The others, preparing to rise, were thrust back into their seats.

It was platform three of Vienna's Südbahnhof, Train Station South. The train had come to the end of the line. The passengers pushed against each other, each eager to be first off the train. It was late, but everywhere was commotion and hurry.

Rawenduzy had deposited his luggage next to him. He stood in the midst of the hubbub, relaxed and calm. It was strange, but he felt an unusual familiarity. "The Lovely Nights of Vienna," was the refrain of a song sung by the famous Egyptian actress As Mahan. Wiriya had probably listened to it a hundred times. How often had he secretly dreamed of those Vienna nights? How he had wished he would some day experience them.

Was he imagining this? It did not seem real, such bliss. But he had made it.

The two black hands of the big clock in the station jolted Rawenduzy from his reverie. He picked up his luggage and hurried across the hall. The night was fading rapidly, and he needed a place to sleep.

A small hotel across the street seemed appropriate. He rang the doorbell, and after a long wait a sleepy night clerk opened the door and distrustfully sized up the stranger. Wiriya hoped that the man knew at least some English. Luckily, he did. The man quickly checked Wiriya into a room, handed him a key, and disappeared with shuffling steps down the hall, wishing Wiriya a pleasant good night.

Wiriya Rawenduzy dragged his two suitcases and brown leather bag to the second floor and dropped into bed, exhausted from the long journey. The room was tiny and austerely furnished. A grey iron bed stood in the middle of the room, and the yellowed curtains sagged from the curtain rod, on one side even having come loose entirely. The worm-eaten closet had seen better days and seemed ashamed of its shabby looks. Before the war, Wiriya found out later, it had stood in an elegant villa in Hietzing, an upscale classical district in western Vienna.

The air in the room was stuffy and stale. Wiriya rose from the bed and opened a small window overlooking a narrow courtyard. Cool, fresh air streamed into the room. On a table, there was a pitcher with cold water and a washbasin. There was no running water. Wiriya swiftly undressed to bathe, and a short while later, refreshed and cleaned from head to toe, he changed into light pajamas and took care to dump the dirty water into a bucket in the room. He stretched his tired body over the bed and closed his eyes. A feeling of happiness mingled with fear overtook him. He slipped into a dreamless sleep, thinking only that he must rest to prepare for a new day. For a new life.

It was a warm August day, and bright rays of sunshine fell on the courtyard of a small hotel near Vienna's Südbahnhof. The morning had long since broken, and the hotel had long since come to life, but the young man in room eleven was still asleep. It was close to nine o'clock when Wiriya awoke. His stomach had awakened him. How long had it been since he had eaten? He remembered that he still had a few apples somewhere in his luggage. He found one and munched on it as he put on his pants and shirt. Wiriya loved fruit. Bread and fruit. How do you say that in German, he wondered.

He grabbed his wallet and pocket dictionary and was on his way. Downstairs the clerk explained in broken English and exaggerated gestures that Wiriya could have breakfast at the hotel if he so desired, at an extra charge of course. Wiriya gladly agreed. Cost what it may, he had to celebrate his first day in Vienna.

The clerk led Wiriya Rawenduzy into a sunlit dining room. In the room, there were five small tables covered with white tablecloths, and chairs decorated by cheap pink covers. A stout middle-aged woman, obviously unused to such niceties as changing her apron daily, greeted the young man cordially.

"Good morning! Did you sleep well? You picked a wonderful day. Now you must eat something. I'll get you coffee and bread. Unfortunately, there is no butter, but I will get you some margarine and jam. Will that suit you?"

She did not truly expect an answer; by the time she had finished talking she had already disappeared behind a narrow glass door into the kitchen. Her smile was friendly and etched two dimples deep into her face. Aside from "bread", Wiriya had not understood a single word. He waited in anticipation, wondering what he would get, and his glance wandered through the room. A crucifix hung over the entrance. Two pictures of waterfalls and hunters decorated the otherwise bare walls. Wiriya felt carefree and began to ponder what he should do after breakfast. Should he call immediately? No, he still wanted to rest a bit. Lost in thought he stroked his head, which was covered by a thick mop of hair. Suddenly he remembered. He had the address and phone number of the Krammers, a Viennese family who had agreed to help him get started in Vienna. Before he made contact with them he had to have a haircut. After all, he had to make a good first impression.

"Bon Appetite!" said the hostess. "I have added a croissant." She disappeared again. On the plate before Wiriya were three slices of bread, a croissant, a large mug of malt coffee with milk, two lumps of sugar, some margarine, and a tiny plate of apricot jam. This was Wiriya's first meal in a foreign country, and he savored each bite. He was in absolutely no hurry.

After breakfast, he set out to search for a barbershop in the vicinity, and after a short search he met with success on a nearby side street. Elated, Wiriya opened the door. But what was this? The barber's chair was occupied, and a young, blond woman was winding the gray hair of the customer stylishly into a bun. A female barber? And blond and pretty nonetheless. The young Iraqi was completely unprepared for this. In his country, only men, black-haired, older men worked as barbers.

The hairdresser motioned for Wiriya to take a seat. She explained that she was still busy with another customer, and that he would have to wait a few minutes. He did not understand a single word, but watching this young woman made up for the time spent waiting. After approximately fifteen minutes the old customer left, quite satisfied, and the hairdresser turned to Wiriya. Unfortunately, she did not understand English. Wiriya had no other choice but to use gestures to communicate to her that she should cut his hair short. She smiled charmingly and launched her scissors and comb into action. In ten minutes, she was finished, and Wiriya was overjoyed, not only with her beauty but also with his new haircut.

The next day Wiriya Rawenduzy called Mrs. Krammer. Spontaneous and happy that he had arrived safely, she invited him to have lunch with her and her family that very day. She was a pen pal of a relative of his father. When she had learned in a recent letter that Wiriya could use her help and support upon his arrival in Vienna, she had immediately agreed to assist him. It was excellent luck for Wiriya, because the Krammer family lived in the Third District, only a twenty-minute walk from his hotel.

Everything went smoothly. He received clear directions to the house, delivered in perfect English. At twelve noon sharp he rang he doorbell. Mrs. Kramer and her two daughters, Sissy and Marlene, gave Wiriya a warm welcome, and their unprejudiced openness and immediate affection laid the cornerstone for a lifelong friendship.

For lunch, he was served plum dumplings coated with breadcrumbs and powdered sugar, a Viennese specialty. Mrs. Krammer put four dumplings on the plate of the young man and wished him a good appetite. It must be understood that in the Middle East sweet dishes are never served as a main course, so as Wiriya started to eat he was confused by the lack of a main dish. He was certainly not used to so much sweet food.

As he ate, he answered many questions about his journey and about his future studies in Vienna. Mrs. Krammer promised to help Wiriya find a room close to the University of Vienna. She would check the ads in the local newspaper after lunch.

With the utmost effort, Wiriya managed to finish the dumplings, and the lady of the house asked him if he had liked the meal. Wishing to be polite, Wiriya nodded. Promptly, Mrs. Krammer piled four more dumplings on his plate. In the Krammer household, the guest was king, and Wiriya should not return to his hotel hungry.

Since that day, Dr. Rawenduzy has never again done two things. First, he has not touched those sugared plum dumplings even a single time. Second, he has never again said that he liked food if he did not, even out of politeness.

The following days were extremely hectic. They began to search for an apartment, but soon they ran into trouble. While many landlords were advertising rooms to rent, far fewer actually had them available once they saw that the prospective tenant was an Iraqi with a dark complexion. Even in those days, latent animosity towards foreigners was already showing its face in Vienna. Nevertheless, Wiriya and Mrs. Krammer were finally successful, and Wiriya was able to rent a room on the fourth floor of an apartment building on Schoenborngasse, in Vienna's Eighth District. He had found a new home.

The older daughter of Mrs. Krammer, Marlene, patiently began to explain German to the young man – the masculine article "der", the feminine article "die", the neutral article "das" – but sentence construction and articles became hopelessly entangled, creating more problems than solutions. Wiriya's homework, dutifully written, was in most cases completely wrong, and soon Wiriya became desperate. He wanted to study medicine, not waste his precious time on the grammatical rules of "Der, Die, and Das". He decided to concentrate on physics, and began to skip his German lessons with Marlene. She protested vigorously, but he was determined to get ahead in his studies, and to pass his tests. Knowledge of German grammar did not seem essential to him.

Study, study, study – often up to twelve hours a day – this was now his life. This was his future. He had never lost site of the goal of becoming a medical doctor, now nothing and no one could keep him from following his dream. He had suffered too many setbacks and too much injustice to quit now. He was ready to fight, for himself and for his people.

Kurdish Student Congress. Germany. 1961

Kurdish students in Baghdad with General Qassim. 1961

Dr. Rawenduzy's graduation in Vienna. November 1961

Chase the Gray Out of Your Everyday

I always felt the name they gave us was wrong. Emigrants. It means 'One who departs his country to settle elsewhere, possibly forever'. However, we did not just 'depart' our country of our own free will. We did not just travel to another country to settle there, possibly forever. We fled. We are refugees, exiles. We have no home, and the country that accepted us could never be anything more to us than a place of exile.

Bertolt Brecht

Many months passed. Wiriya Rawenduzy studied day and night. In Physics, he passed with distinction. In Chemistry, he passed with an A. In Anatomy, he also passed with distinction. He did all of this just in time to qualify for an extended residency permit, allowing him to continue his studies.

By this time, an Iraqi student organization had been founded in Vienna. It had strong ties to Communism. The group met in a small café on Schwarzspanierstrasse, close to the Institute of Anatomy. Iraqis frequented this café, and from time to time Kurdish students could be found there as well. Contacts were made, addresses and telephone numbers exchanged.

At the same time in Baghdad, a coup enabled General Abdul Karim Qassim to rise to power. The royal family was executed, and the acting Prime Minister assassinated, his body hung from a pole and displayed in public.

Again the Kurds entertained hopes. They had always been told that the imperialists were responsible for their misery, and now one could be optimistic. An autonomous and united Kurdistan was still the goal, a country with full rights for its people. This included the right of the Kurdish people to live according to their own culture, and to conduct their affairs in their own language.

Dr. Rawenduzy with nurses and doctors. Kaiser-Franz-Josef Hospital, 1965

The year was 1958, the year of the revolution. The movement of Kurdish students residing abroad had begun, and Wiriya Rawenduzy was one of its founders. The leaders of this movement felt Europe should take up the issue of the Kurds anew, and should become sympathetic to the Kurdish cause. Congresses were organized, and among other things, Rawenduzy acted as Vice President of one of them.

However, the Iraqi student organization was ready. They let it be known that anyone who even hinted at, let alone spoke of a Kurdish nation would be considered a traitor and a supporter of imperialism. They declared that anyone advocating Kurdish nationalism could only be working for the ruin of Iraq, and such separatism had to be vigorously opposed.

The central Kurdish party continued to demand an autonomous state within the framework of the Republic of Iraq. However, Rawenduzy and his supporters wanted more. They criticized the constitution of Iraq because one section of it,

Article 3, stipulated that Iraq was a part of the Arabic Nation. The Kurds had two problems with this. First, the Iraqi Kurds considered themselves part of the Kurdish nation, not the Arab nation. Second, one could not proclaim a country such as Iraq to be part of a nation. Thus, Rawenduzy believed that Article 3 had to be considered a linguistic error.

In 1961, Dr. Ismet Cherif Vanly, considered by most to be the President of the Kurdish Committee to Defend Kurdish Rights, expressed this criticism of Article 3 while participating in a Congress of the International Student Union. His interpretation of Article 3 spread like wildfire, presenting a new vision as well as new information. Of course, Vanly's remarks were published in the newspaper of the Kurdish Democratic Party, and this was the last straw in that party's relations with the representatives of General Qassim's government. "Separatist, tendentious," the Kurdish movement was called. An ill wind had begun to blow.

Vanly had spoken continuously about Kurdistan as a nation with several regions – North, South, and West Kurdistan. This was historically correct. Iraq had once been a part of the Ottoman Empire, which the major world powers had divided at the close of World War I. From this division, they had created states according to their liking, and Faysal, originally from Saudi Arabia, was proclaimed by the British to be the King of Iraq.

Moreover, in 1921 England and Iraq reached an agreement on the Kurdish question, in which the Kurds were promised an autonomous government, a promise that was never truly fulfilled. This was the lead-up to the events of 1961, in which the Kurds under their leader Mulla Mustafa Barzani fought against the government of General Qassim.

Since the eighteenth century, there have been constant Kurdish uprisings. All of them, including the last one in 1991, were put down brutally and cruelly. In March 1988, in Halabdja, Saddam Hussein had 5,000 Kurds killed within a few hours. These included people of all ages, from babies to old men, and all died an excruciating death by means of poison gas.

By the early sixties, Wiriya Rawenduzy had finished his studies in Vienna. In 1961, he graduated with a degree in Medical Sciences from the University of Vienna. He emerged from his studies obsessed with a burning ambition, fortified by an iron will, driven by stubborn perseverance and gifted with extraordinary intelligence. He had succeeded in his goal of becoming a doctor. However, he had not yet reached his ultimate goal. This young man from the wilds of Kurdistan knew that his will demanded of him still more.

He wanted to help. He wanted to ease misery. He wanted to serve his people as a physician. Nothing and no one would prevent him from accomplishing this.

In spite of his enormous efforts in his studies, Rawenduzy had become more and more the focal point of the Kurds' political opposition abroad. Soon the trio of Valy, Ing. Saadi Dizayee, and Rawenduzy were ordered by the Kurdish organizations to form a committee, and were endorsed to act as official and legal representatives of the Kurdish resistance. Kurdish resistance groups were also being founded in other countries in Europe and the groups were attempting to cooperate with each other. They hoped to draw attention to the prevailing abuses in Kurdistan, and were ready to fight in any way they could against the dictatorship back home. The desire of the Kurdish people for a Kurdish identity was legitimate. They believed that democratic structures and the autonomy those structures would create should lay the foundation for the unity of future generations, a unity which would promote and serve individual inner self-awareness.

Unfortunately, the Kurds have a tradition. They are a nation of tribes, and generally, each tribal leader wants to rule all of the other tribes. Even in the 1960's, tribal rivalries created tensions, which caused vicious conflicts, which on the surface seemed to solve the issues when one tribe or another won.

However, this constant conflict made the job of the Iraqi regime quite easy. When the tribal disputes flared up, those at the helm of the government could simply take advantage of the moment to step in and bring law and order to the lawless Kurds. On the surface, this might sound good, but what it really meant was that any flickering of democracy could be nipped in the bud by cruel totalitarian methods. All political, social, and cultural life was regimented, subdued, or forbidden by force. Arbitrary actions against Kurds were (and still are) high on the agenda of the Iraqi government. Frequently individual officials could be responsible for the death of some hundred people.

Thus, the Kurds abroad were considered a horde of uneducated, fanatical warmongers, chaotic rioters who pretended they wanted autonomy in order to gain power for their respective tribes. Loud demonstrations in European cities often met with little public sympathy, for the public was not aware of the true problems of this suppressed people. In fact, many a European believed the Kurds themselves were at fault for their situation. Nevertheless, the leaders of the Kurdish organizations generally managed to succeed in finding open ears among the representatives of foreign nations.

Rawenduzy did not idle away his time. He organized congresses, and wrote publications, leaflets, and letters to the editor. His intentions were on one hand to promote the rights of the Kurdish people and on the other hand, to criticize the brutality of the Iraqi government against the Kurds. He made repeated contact with Austrian politicians of different parties and attempted to make them see the violation of human rights that was occurring in Iraq. Some politicians showed interest. Some contemplated lending their support.

Meanwhile the Iraqi Secret Service had learned of the far-reaching activities of Wiriya Rawenduzy, and soon the Iraqi

Minister of Foreign Affairs sent Dr. Rawenduzy an official letter. The letter said that Dr. Rawenduzy was herewith stripped of his Iraqi citizenship. No reasons were given. To make matters worse, the postscript of the letter stated that a warrant had been issued for Dr. Rawenduzy's arrest.

Rawenduzy was able to read between the lines of such a letter, and immediately he realized that his situation had become extremely dangerous. In Iraq, critics of the regime were often silenced by execution. Abroad there was assassination and contracted murder.

But this was not to be the end of the bad news. Soon Dr. Rawenduzy found out that the Austrian authorities had decided not to extend his residency permit.

But why? The last straw for the Austrian government had come not long before, when the Kurdish politician Jalal Talabani had come to Vienna after a visit with Egyptian President Nasser, and had held a press conference in which he declared that negotiations between the Kurds and the government of Baghdad had failed. Now Austria wanted to get rid of a highly politically active Kurdish physician. The state police informed Rawenduzy that he had to leave Austria within forty-eight hours. Chaos reigned in Rawenduzy's life. The Kurd informed his friends of the bad news, said goodbye to everyone he could reach, and gave notice of his departure to his employer, the hospital in Wiener Neustadt.

However, in the meantime the Minister of the Interior, Franz Olah, had been informed of the Rawenduzy case, and of Dr. Rawenduzy's imminent expulsion. When he heard the news, Olah could not believe it. He knew Dr. Rawenduzy. Of course, he understood why Dr. Rawenduzy had lost his citizenship. He understood why Rawenduzy's passport was no longer valid. Without citizenship or a passport, he understood why the Austrian authorities had denied Rawenduzy an extension of his residency permit. It was, legally, absolutely correct… and from a human standpoint utterly abominable.

Olah acted immediately and completely unbureaucratically. Using his power as Minster of the Interior, he ordered Dr. Rawenduzy's expulsion to be lifted at once, and his contract at the hospital in Wiener Neustadt to be guaranteed. End of debate.

Rawenduzy was touched. Justice had won. Franz Olah had demonstrated that a commitment to humanity was not always lip service. He sought out Mr. Olah to express his gratitude, but Olah explained that he had merely done his duty. It was his duty to help others, and if need be to protect them. That was it.

In 1964, Wiriya Rawenduzy married a Viennese woman, became an Austrian citizen, and settled down. Slowly, he got used to the idea that he would not be able to return home and use his medical skills there. His Kurdish soul was in an uproar, but his sharp intellect suppressed such feelings.

For family reasons Rawenduzy changed workplaces from Wiener Neustadt to Vienna and resumed work at Kaiser-Franz-Josef Hospital. In 1968, he successfully completed his specialized training in internal medicine. Gradually, he tried to withdraw from politics.

However, his Kurdish friends were still counting on their boss. He received requests from Iraqi Kurdistan to return home and help found the medical school at Sulaymania University. Physicians were urgently needed there. Medical care for the poor and woe-stricken population was inadequate. Rawenduzy was needed to help set up a health center and to oversee medical training at the university. The situation was serious: initial health care was dreadful and consequently infant mortality was extremely high.

Rawenduzy pondered this request extensively. Iraqi Kurdistan was still not an autonomous territory. There had been no improvement for the Kurds. The Iraqi government continued to violate human rights, and the warrant for Rawenduzy's arrest had not been lifted.

There were just too many arguments against returning. Besides there was now a private reason to stay in Vienna – his first son, Simko, had just been born.

After considering all this, Rawenduzy composed a letter to the Kurdish leadership spelling out his views and making specific requests, which he hoped would lead to a positive outcome of the matter at hand. They understood, and the project was postponed indefinitely.

Several years later the health care project came to the fore again and Rawenduzy was approached and asked to serve as an advisor or even to support the project more actively. He decided to undertake the task if certain conditions were met. This time he addressed his letter directly to the government of Iraq.

He requested that the warrant for his arrest be lifted, and that the Iraqi government officially recognize his medical training, including his specialized training in Internal Medicine. The Iraqi government's reply bore the signatures of three Iraqi ministers. First, said the letter, a committee would be formed to study the certificates from Austria. The members of this committee would decide whether his medical studies and his specialized training in Vienna would be recognized in Iraq. However, the members of the Iraqi government were not authorized to make a decision on the matter of his arrest warrant.

Rawenduzy got the picture. A return to Kurdistan was impossible. The Kurdish physician would not take such risks. Anyway, his second son, Alan, had been born, and this was yet another reason to remain longer in Vienna.

Responsibility was – and still is to this day – one of the highest priorities in the life of Dr. Wiriya Rawenduzy. He puts his life in the service of human beings; he seeks to help them. He aided the Austrian population greatly through his involvement in the blood donor program of the Austrian Red Cross. He initiated and executed numerous collections and shipments of medicine to Iraqi Kurdistan over a period of thirty years. Often this Kurdish doctor, when treating a patient hard-pressed for money or without health insurance, was known to forget to make out the bill, or to accidentally give away the required medicine free of charge. Because of these and many other acts of service, many people in Austria might very well owe Dr. Rawenduzy their lives.

He had always known that his tireless work for the good of humankind was only a drop in the bucket. Nevertheless, he possessed a deeply humanitarian attitude, a respect for life, and eternally high morale, and consequently he was able to continuously put the welfare of others first. He would not ignore social mores or state regulations, but Rawenduzy succeeded balancing morality and legality so he could make decisions according to ethical values.

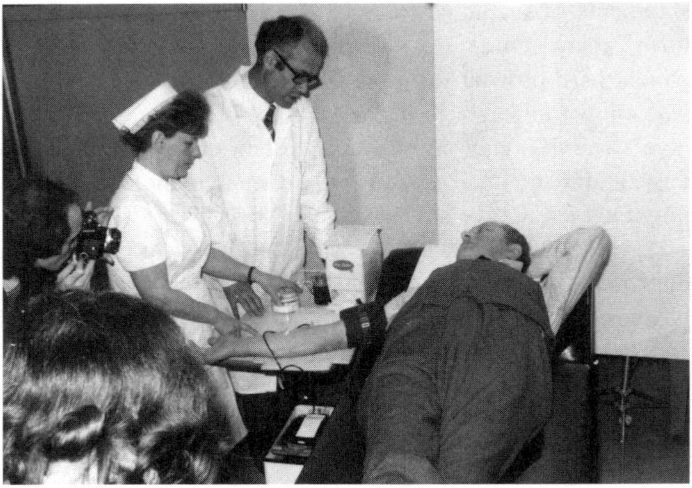

Austrian Chancellor Bruno Kreisky donates blood. May 8, 1974.

“The Promise”: The Austrian Chancellor bids farewell to Dr. Rawenduzy

Calm Blood

It was about eleven o'clock in the morning and a cool wind blew through Vienna. The city was a picture of vibrant activity. People ran back and forth, cars wove between streetcars and buses, and traffic lights glowed their irradiant light. Red, Red-Yellow, Green-Blink-Yellow, Red, Green.

It was an ordinary day in May. Streetcars glided majestically through the streets on their tracks as they did every day, but today something was different. The streetcars were decorated with small Red Cross flags. When they came to a halt, it almost looked as though they were proud of their new accoutrements.

Through the traffic snaked a shiny black limousine. It was accompanied by two "White Mice", elite members of the Vienna special police force who dressed in tight leather overalls and roared through the streets in heavy motorcycles.

At the same time, across town at the headquarters of the Austrian Red Cross, there was great hustle and bustle. The elegant house which served as the Red Cross's headquarters was expecting a visit by Austrian Chancellor Dr. Bruno Kreisky. It was International Red Cross Day, and Dr. Kreisky intended to donate blood.

The date was May 8, 1974. All day, the Red Cross staff had been rushing about preparing for the event. Early that day, the Secretary General of the Austrian Red Cross, Hans Polster, had excitedly called the head of the blood bank, Dr. Wiriya Rawenduzy, to discuss the details of the event. On which bed exactly would Kreisky lie while donating blood? Which nurse would assist Rawenduzy? Where would the journalists and press photographers be allowed to stand? Should Kreisky be addressed while he was donating blood? If so, which topics would be suitable?

The answers to these questions varied in content and strength of opinion, but to one question, the answer was absolute. It went without saying that the doctor who would attend to Kreisky would be Rawenduzy. It had to be Rawenduzy personally.

There was no doubt in his mind, said Polster, as to who should tackle this delicate matter, or as to which of the doctors at the Austrian Red Cross had his full confidence. Rawenduzy would be filmed live as he inserted the needle into the Chancellor's vein, so each move had to be precise – the taking of the blood pressure, the attaching of the elastic bandage, the painless insertion of the needle. Under no circumstances should there be a hemorrhage. The blood should flow freely into the receptacle.

Even the slightest risk was to be avoided. At that time, due to the recent death of President Franz Jonas, Kreisky was not only Federal Chancellor but also acting President of Austria. Everything depended on Rawenduzy now. Polster was counting on him, fully aware that the reputation of the Austrian Red Cross rested in the hands of one reliable physician.

That day Rawenduzy was on duty, just as he was every other day. He was, as always, correct and precise. First, he conversed briefly with the head nurse, and told her that a slight, almost insignificant gesture by him would indicate that the blood donation was to stop immediately. She should not ask questions; she should simply do it. Of course, the head nurse understood this without being told. She knew her boss very well, and she held him in the highest esteem because of his expertise.

It was agreed that the bed would be placed in the middle of the room to allow more space for the accompanying police and press. However, it was important to Rawenduzy that a certain distance be maintained between the renowned politician and the spectators. He alone would remain at the side of the famous blood donor, as a physician, as the man responsible for the Chancellor's health.

But not, in any way, as a former political activist.

Outside the Red Cross building, the driver of the large black limousine slowly reduced its speed and pulled up to the curve on the right side of the street. The headquarters of the Red Cross was a building of a rich yellow-gold color much like that of the Palace of Schönbrunn, the former summer residence of the Habsburg Monarchs. The headquarters' appearance was striking, and the building was hard to overlook. Above the house, a white flag with a red cross in the center flew in the wind. Police cars lined the building's main entrance. On the sidewalk, uniformed men stood guard, their badges golden and shining in the sun. There were gentlemen in dark, tailor-made suits, and onlookers leaned close to each other to whisper in each other's ears. It seemed that someone important was expected today.

The official limousine of the Austrian Chancellor had come to a standstill. The White Mice shielded the car from the traffic, and traffic police stopped the other automobiles. The safety of the politician would not be put at risk for any reason.

The door of the limousine opened. The crowd began to whisper, then to applaud loudly. Yes, it was he. Kreisky emerged from the limousine and faced the cheering people. A soft smile appeared on his well-known face.

The Viennese loved 'their Kreisky'. The Chancellor's popularity was immense. He graciously thanked the people and shook many hands, his bodyguards standing at extreme alert. Hans Polster approached the Chancellor, greeted him respectfully, and ushered him into the foyer of the Red Cross headquarters. The staff had gathered in the hall and in front of the staircase. Everyone wanted to see the Chancellor in person for once in his life.

The Chancellor and his entourage took the stairs to the first floor, pausing repeatedly so Kreisky could ask questions and listen as the Secretary General explained things. Kreisky was a master conversationalist, while at the same time he often seemed aloof and spoke in a way that could feel both distant and sharp. People around him often felt uneasy, and he rarely showed emotion.

The delegation was absorbed in conversation the whole way up the stairs, and soon it had reached the hub of the blood bank on the first floor. Everywhere were members of the press and high-ranking police officers.

Night nurses scurried by in blue and white outfits with small white caps secured tightly to their hair. They cast short, discrete glances at the prominent people. None of the nurses envied their boss, and they wondered if today, finally, he might for once be a bit excited. However, they did not really believe he was. They knew Dr. Rawenduzy. They knew he was always serious, always correct, and that he never showed any emotion.

The Secretary General entered the room first. Rawenduzy smiled, almost imperceptibly, when the Chancellor shook his hand. They exchanged a few words, the Chancellor's bodyguard remaining in the background. Journalists tried to place questions to Kreisky, but he ignored them and concentrated on donating blood. Rawenduzy assisted the Chancellor as he took off his jacket, and Kreisky rolled up his right sleeve. Then Kreisky lay down and the Kurdish physician took his blood pressure.This was mere routine. The glare of flashbulbs lit up the room, which smelled of disinfectant.

The room was full and time was short, so Rawenduzy skipped the routine questions as to any illnesses or ailments the potential donor might have. Then he checked the blood pressure reading.

Too high. The words flashed through his mind and impacted on his conscience. Around them, the onlookers were talking noisily, their conversation creating a din and drowning out Rawenduzy's faint question to Kreisky:

"Do you know that your blood pressure is too high?"

Surprised, Kreisky answered that he did not.

Many years later, when Bruno Kreisky and Wiriya Rawenduzy had become friends, the politician remembered this scene, and remarked that Rawenduzy had been the first doctor to alert him to this problem. Because of this, he had undergone targeted medical tests and blood analysis.

The head nurse stood two steps behind Rawenduzy. She handed him the needle. Kreisky put his left hand under his head and, seeming relaxed, looked with interest at Rawenduzy. The Chancellor had only heard Rawenduzy speak a few sentences, but he easily recognized that the doctor did not come from Central Europe.

Rawenduzy found a vein and inserted the needled without causing Kreisky the least bit of pain. Soon the blood was flowing slowly into the plastic bag.

The cameras began to click again, but not one of the journalists, photographers, or television reporters addressed Kreisky. They conversed quietly, yet did not take their eyes off the important donor. Kreisky was looking straight into Rawenduzy's eyes.

"Where do you come from?" he suddenly asked.

He received a polite reply. "From Iraqi Kurdistan."

Kreisky seemed pleased with this, and said something that sought to draw a parallel between Rawenduzy and Herbert von Karajan, who had also had foreign roots and had become world-famous.

The doctor made a modest hand gesture. What did he have to do with fame, he thought. To compare him with the gifted maestro was rather odd.

The politician smiled and remarked that several well-known Austrian personalities had forefathers from other countries. He seemed serious.

One third of the plastic bag had already been filled. Rawenduzy did not want to take any risks. He motioned to the head nurse as they had agreed, and stopped the flow of blood. Complications had to be avoided, and no one would notice that only a third of the plastic bag had been filled. Then the wound was attended to, and since bleeding was out of the question, a special bandage was affixed to Kreisky's arm.

By this time, Kreisky had begun to interview the Kurdish doctor regarding his position on several political issues. Among other things, the Chancellor wanted to know about the Middle East, which was as much a hotbed then as it is now.

Rawenduzy tried to avoid talking about politics and stick to his roll as a physician, but the experienced politician insisted. Rawenduzy attempted to withhold his personal opinion and answer only in general terms, but Kreisky was not to be dissuaded and encouraged him to open up. Rawenduzy warned the Chancellor that he might not like his replies. Kreisky waved this off.

Rawenduzy began to talk. In the conversation that followed, he and the Chancellor discussed most of the highly explosive contemporary issues concerning the Arab world. They discussed Israel and Palestine. They discussed the peace agreement between President Sadat of Egypt and Prime Minister Begin of Israel. They discussed the position of Iraq in the affairs of the region. Finally, they reached the issue of the Kurds, who were the largest population without autonomy. Kreisky noted that this situation could potentially spark another conflict in the Middle East, and he encouraged the doctor to forward to his office a detailed report on the Kurdish issue. Rawenduzy promised to compile the requested report and submit it to the Chancellor.

During most of the conversation, Kreisky let Rawenduzy speak, which felt like a great privilege to Rawenduzy; and the doctor made good use of the opportunity to express his opinions. He felt, instinctively, that the charismatic politician appreciated his honest comments.

Kreisky pulled his sleeve down over the bandage and got to his feet in a good mood. The reporters in attendance gave him a round of applause, and took some more photos. The

Chancellor's bodyguards accompanied Kreisky to the main hall, and refreshments were served. The Chancellor was very relaxed, and he sipped a glance of orange juice and conversed with those around him. His personal secretary glanced nervously at his watch. Time was pressing, and the next appointment was to follow.

However, the Chancellor had apparently been impressed with his conversation with Rawenduzy, for he decided to return to the doctor. He took Rawenduzy's hand, shook it firmly, and thanked him for his frankness. Rawenduzy promised to be at Kreisky's disposal whenever he needed him.

Little did the Kurd know that such an opportunity would present itself no later than the following year.

This meeting between Rawenduzy and Kreisky was the beginning of a long term, if loose, friendship. A few days after Kreisky's visit to the Red Cross Blood Bank, he received his Red Cross Donors Identification Card, signed personally by Dr. Rawenduzy. The Chancellor carried the card in his pocket wherever he went.

Months later Kreisky and Rawenduzy saw each other at a reception. Rawenduzy, always polite, introduced himself as if they had never met. Kreisky, however, shook Rawenduzy's hand, reached into his pocket, pulled out his Red Cross ID Card, pointed to Rawenduzy's signature, proclaimed, "Oh, I know you well!", and flashed a winning smile at the doctor.

Somewhat embarrassed, Rawenduzy apologized. Kreisky waved it off and wasted no time in leveling at Rawenduzy some very specific political questions. Soon they were engaged in a lively discussion.

In October 1981, Anwar Sadat was murdered by an Egyptian soldier during a military parade. Many years after the assassination, while Kreisky and Rawenduzy were in attendance at an OPEC reception in Vienna, Kreisky asked Rawenduzy why so many years before the attack, indeed in that first year of their acquaintance, 1974, Rawenduzy had believed such an attack on Sadat would occur.

"On one hand the Arabs were not ready for this peace agreement and its consequences," said Rawenduzy. "Unfortunately, making political concessions and realizing them are two very different pairs of shoes. On the other hand, the tragedy happened because Israel and her settlers had been disregarding the human beings in the occupied territories, and that is the real cause of the tragedy."

There, at the OPEC reception, after the assassination, Dr. Bruno Kreisky nodded pensively. How tragically correct this physician from faraway Kurdistan had been back in 1974.

Kreisky is recognized as an accomplished international politician, and during his career he stood up for more mutual understanding in the Middle East conflict, a position that met with criticism, especially from Israel. Nevertheless, Kreisky continued his policy of advocating humanity in all things, without exception.

Dr. Wiriya Rawenduzy has become a patronizing member of the Bruno Kreisky Forum and regularly attends lectures and receptions held at the former Kreisky Villa in Doebling, a district in Vienna. Rawenduzy maintains his political independence, yet he cherishes the ineffaceable memory of Bruno Kreisky, the brilliant politician, extraordinary human being, and most importantly, Dr. Rawenduzy's friend.

The OPEC Psycho: A Man Sets Off

It was three days before Christmas, and the gifts for the children still needed to be wrapped. Ah, the children. Just thinking about them, the face of streetcar conductor Josef Pokorny lit up. Pepi, Anni, and Fredi – they were his pride. As a family they had little living space; they lived in a small, one-room apartment in Simmering. However, who worried about things like that? The children played mostly in the yard outside the building. When Josef was off duty the family spent a large portion of their time outside. In the winter, they went sledding or went out to the Old Danube, frozen at that time of year, and slid across the ice. In the summer, they went swimming at Heustadlwasser. Josef's wife Mizzi would pack a picnic basket with breaded veal cutlets and potato salad, and there was cool beer as a treat for the parents and raspberry soda for the children.

Next stop, Schottentor. He needed to concentrate. It was shortly before noon, and the Ringstrasse, one of Vienna's main boulevards, was full of traffic. Inside the streetcar, people pushed against each other to get to the exits. Most had pulled their caps over their faces and put up the collars of their overcoats. It was bitter cold and the snow cracked under people's shoes. Pokorny noticed that several of the passengers did not speak German. He wondered what they were talking about. He watched them as they got off the streetcar. The men were about thirty years old, and one of them was dressed in a stylish leather jacket and wore a beret. The men carried bags, their hands gripping the handles tightly. There was one woman. She was rather small, and was wrapped in a long skirt that she had to lift when she got out of the streetcar. She was well-protected from the cold by an elegant leather coat with a fur collar, and she wore a heavy shawl.

Pokorny heard the signal and put the streetcar in motion. He looked at the big public clock on the other side of the Ringstrasse. It was 11:20 AM.

It was a Sunday, and Dr. Wiriya Rawenduzy was on call. On weekends, he and five other specialists provided medical care to members of international organizations such as the Atomic Energy Commission and UNIDO. Since mobile phones were not available to most people in 1975, it was customary for the physician on duty to wait at home for incoming calls. That morning Rawenduzy had comfortably settled down by the telephone. He was reading with great interest the reports in the daily newspapers on the OPEC conference scheduled to take place in Vienna that day.

His thoughts began to wander. His younger brother, Zozek, had been head of the OPEC legal department from 1970 to 1972. Through him, Rawenduzy had met several OPEC employees, had become the physician of some of them, and had even befriended a few. Zozek Rawenduzy had studied law in Baghdad. He had wanted to study international law, so he undertook and completed further legal studies at the Sorbonne in Paris, where he got married and chose the French capital as his permanent home. The two brothers had not seen each other for a long time, and they had not had regular contact. What a pity, Rawenduzy thought. At this moment, for some reason, he deeply regretted the lack of contact.

The telephone did not ring the entire morning of December 21, 1975. Perhaps it would be a quiet Sunday after all. Rawenduzy put down his newspaper and got up from his comfortable armchair. It was shortly before noon. He decided it was time to turn on the radio and listen to the news.

The voice of the commentator broke into the room. However, what was he talking about? Rawenduzy could make no sense of it. Agitated, he turned the knobs of the radio to get better reception. What was it that had just happened? The reporter seemed to be stammering his words, and Rawenduzy struggled to follow. This could not be true. He turned the volume of the radio up as high as it could go.

An attack!? OPEC? Hostages? Some assumed to be dead. Rawenduzy was pacing frantically in his room. What should he do?

He knew that the physician responsible for the OPEC staff was Dr. Osama Hamid. However, hadn't Dr. Hamid mentioned that he might be skiing this weekend? Dr. Rawenduzy grabbed the telephone. He knew his friend Hamid's number by heart. He dialed, and it rang, and rang, seconds seeming like hours. Why was nobody answering? Someone just had to answer. But the phone continued to ring, seeming not to care at all about what the caller thought. Furious and disappointed, Rawenduzy slammed down the receiver.

The voice from the radio screamed into Dr. Rawenduzy's room. Eleven oil ministers had been taken hostage. Rawenduzy listened, breathless. Several attackers had entered OPEC Headquarters and had immediately opened fire. One of the police officers on duty had tried to wrest the submachine gun from the presumed leader of the terrorists, and that officer had paid for his deed with his life.

The criminals had continued mercilessly on their path of death, and soon, there was absolute chaos in the building. The killers had taken the police officers by surprise, and the officers had had absolutely no chance against their brutality. It was clear that these criminals were a dangerous commando unit. What did they really have in mind? Which demands would they make? Or did they only wish to murder, in order to prove to the world that they had the power to kill?

Up until now, Vienna had been spared terrorist attacks. It had been a quiet metropolis. Now it was having a rude awakening. Foreign killers had destroyed the city's complacency on the last Sunday before Christmas Eve. No one knew how to handle the situation. All were paralyzed.

Like the others, Rawenduzy could not comprehend this gruesome news. He had already experienced much evil in his life, but not here, not in Vienna. This city had been almost an oasis within the never-ending disaster of worldwide conflicts. Despite having an internationally known Chancellor who was actively engaged in peace efforts, the city of Vienna was usually involved in nothing more than domestic political drama. But this attack was brutal, and against foreign guests no less, and it had exposed Austria for the first time to an unknown dimension of global terror.

One of the criminals had been shot and seriously wounded. He had been taken by ambulance to the public hospital and was to be operated on within minutes. The voice of the radio announcer was hoarse. It cracked.

Rawenduzy was gripped by inner unrest. You have to help. You are a physician. You speak Arabic. All of these thoughts flashed through his mind. In his mind's eye, he saw the innocent people at the OPEC Headquarters on the Ringstrasse, and instinctively he began to look around the room for his medical supply bag. It was made of soft brown leather, and as he looked at it, it seemed to symbolize tranquility and calmness. It also seemed slightly bored, like it was waiting for today's first mission.

Rawenduzy stopped abruptly. How could he hesitate any longer? Quickly, he put on a warm sweater, took his bag, threw his winter jacket over his arm, and raced to his car. He quickly called "Good-bye" to his family, and was on his way.

Small snowflakes danced on the windows of his car. The windshield wipers were having trouble clearing the windshield. Thank God, there was little traffic on the icy roads of Vienna. Rawenduzy accelerated. He had soon passed Reichsbrücke and the traffic lights were green on Lassallestrasse. Be careful, said his inner voice. He pressed softly on the brake before reaching Praterstern; there was a traffic circle there and he could not afford an accident. He signaled a right turn, switched the windshield wipers to their maximum speed, and turned into Praterstern.

Red. The traffic light stopped the traffic before the Aspernbrücke. It seemed like an eternity before the green light indicated that he could go. Then his spacious car was cruising quietly along the Ringstrasse. Several times the traffic lights forced him to stop, and he had the chance to focus on the latest news on the radio. Five men and one woman had invaded OPEC Headquarters shortly before noon. They had all been armed to the teeth. There identities were a complete mystery.

Rawenduzy looked at his watch. It was 12:30 PM. He slowed down. A huge crowd was blocking the street at the Burgtheater. He had to find parking, and this seemed nearly hopeless just now. Ambulances and patrol cars had formed a chain, and getting through it would be impossible.

Finally, Rawenduzy succeeded in parking his car close to the City Hall. As he opened the door, a bitter, cold wind blew over him. He realized that in the rush to get here he had forgotten to bring his lined gloves.

He quickly pulled on his jacket, grabbed his medical supply bag, and dashed to what seemed to be the center of the action. Did I lock the car? The question flashed through his mind, but he had no time to answer it. He had become a part of the crowd. Spectators loudly discussed the situation, made assumptions, offered comments, and shouted questions in typical Viennese fashion.

"Where do you want to go?"

"Can't you see there has been an attack?"

"You cannot push ahead!"

"Police! This gentleman does not understand a thing!" screeched a shrill voice. A slightly corpulent woman wearing a gigantic fur cap was grasping Rawenduzy's arm. In all the commotion, he had not understood a single word, and he had not for a minute associated the shrill voice with this woman.

Before he could respond, a police officer was at his side. The officer sized Rawenduzy up and asked, "What do you want here?"

Rawenduzy offered a polite but curt reply: "I am a doctor."

"So? The ambulance has already arrived."

Rawenduzy reacted calmly, but he was beginning to get irritated. The police officer requested additional information. Rawenduzy explained again who he was, that he was a doctor, that he worked for international organizations in Vienna and was therefore well known. In the end, Rawenduzy showed his physician's license to prove he was a licensed medical doctor. This was enough for the police officer.

The Kurdish physician proceeded undisturbed to the main entrance of the OPEC Headquarters. There he met Dr. Liebhart, the Chief of Operations. Rawenduzy introduced himself and told Liebhart why he was there. He knew many of the OPEC employees, he explained. In fact, some were his patients. He was on duty today for several international organizations. In addition, he spoke several languages – English, Arabic, Persian, and more – and if needed he could help to translate.

Liebhart was pleased. His face showed tension, but overall he was calm. He thanked Rawenduzy for volunteering to help and said that the police had already tried to get in touch with Dr. Hamid, but unfortunately had been unsuccessful. Apparently, he was not in Vienna, nor was he reachable by phone. Rawenduzy smiled imperceptibly.

Now there was no way back. From this moment on, Rawenduzy was involved. The situation was extremely dangerous. The terrorists had already killed three people in cold blood: a police officer, an OPEC employee, and a Libyan citizen. One of the terrorists had been severely injured by the police and was already being treated at the hospital. Rawenduzy would learn more details shortly.

When he learned the details, he was staggered. The criminals had taken sixty-two hostages. Eleven of them were oil ministers, and fifty-one were OPEC employees. The Kurdish doctor was only familiar with the names of a few of the ministers: Ezzadin Mabruk from Libya, Tonjo Akobo from Nigeria, Ahmed Zaki Al-Yamani from Saudi Arabia, Hernandez Acosta from Venezuela, Mutalib Al-Rasimi from Kuwait, Tayeh Abdul Karim from Iraq, Jamschid Amouzegar from Iran, Ibn Sutowo from Indonesia, Alexis Mboury-Boutzlt from Gabon, Jalme Duenas from Ecuador, and Belaid Abdesselam from Algeria.

Rawenduzy could see no quick end to this nightmare, so he prepared himself for a long night. He had iron self-discipline, and knew it would help him concentrate on his task as a physician. He would never, no matter how great the danger, forget that he was there to help.

"How could this happen? How? Please tell me how this is possible! And in Vienna no less!"

The Algerian Oil Minister Belaid Abdesselam appeared to be losing his self-control. He was verbally bombarding the Chief of Police, accusing him of gross negligence. His face was becoming more and more flushed, the flush now clearly visible despite his dark complexion.

The Algerian was so upset that Dr. Rawenduzy was becoming worried about his blood pressure. Abdesselam's nervousness could lead to dramatic consequences because Abdesselam had been selected by the terrorists to enter the OPEC building and pass on the terrorists' demands.

Rawenduzy glanced at his watch. It had begun to get dark outside, and inside the building there was an eerie silence. The police officers who stood guard in the entrance hall were quiet, their nerves on edge, attempting to remain calm and composed even as their alarmed looks betrayed their inner tension. Luckily, uniforms and bulletproof vests muffled their heartbeats, which must have been pounding.

The Algerian minister returned to the entrance hall, and his arrival intensified the ever-present stress on everyone. He was still agitated, and in his excitement he was speaking Arabic, which none of those in charge understood. Needless to say, this intensified the situation.

What should be done now? How should they react? If they misinterpreted the terrorists' demands, it could jeopardize the lives of more than a hundred people.

Dr. Liebhart knew that the terrorists had little respect for human life, and that they were willing to sacrifice themselves for their cause. He also knew that they would act without scruples or any sense of morality, and that they were likely to behave severely and inhumanely. Liebhart had participated in special police trainings abroad, and so at least in theory he had been exposed to international terrorism. However, it was almost incomprehensible to him that now, shortly before Christmas, the terrorists would select the OPEC Headquarters in Vienna as their target.

He was jolted into reality by a torrent of words from the Algerian. Abdesselam was tense, and the skin on his forehead had contracted into a deep crease.

Then Liebhart overheard someone speaking to Abdesselam, someone who was obviously calming the Algerian down. The man's voice was quiet, and he was speaking Arabic. Liebhart spun around to find Rawenduzy standing behind him, talking to Abdesselam. Rawenduzy had watched the scene, and since he had been the only one present able to understand the minister's outburst, Rawenduzy had begun to translate.

Abdesselam said that he had been selected by the terrorists to act as their mediator, and that he was to deliver the terrorists' demands to the representatives of the Austrian government.

The terrorists wanted a radio, and they wanted to begin to negotiate with competent officials immediately. Abdesselam went on to illustrate the plight of the hostages on the first floor. What he said made the listeners' blood curdle. The majority of the hostages had been handcuffed. The killers were heavily armed, and had placed hand grenades around the room. Abdesselam would be sent back to the hall to deliver additional demands.

Abdesselam concluded that under no circumstances should the police take any action against the terrorists. In this situation, heroism was not called for; it would only lead to dead hostages.

Belaid Abdesselam shot a warning glance around the entrance hall, made a hand gesture to underscore the importance of his words, and slowly ascended the stairs. His posture did not reflect the self-assurance he was trying to project. He seemed scared, in fact terrified, as any person feels when he is trying to protect his life.

Rawenduzy had only come to the OPEC Headquarters to help as a physician, but because of the drama with Abdesselam, he had become the center of attention. He had succeeded in calming down the raging Algerian. Immediately, Liebhart recognized the diplomatic skills of the Kurdish doctor and inwardly thanked him for his presence.

Two of Liebhart's assistants left the building at once to see to the terrorists' demands. As soon as they were outside, a cluster of journalists descended upon them and pressed them for the latest news, which would be passed on to listeners and readers.

Inside the entrance hall, the narrow, dusty porter's box had become the police force's strategic center. This was because it was the location of the only telephone still in operation, the location of telephones being a decisive factor. When the terrorists had attacked, one of them had gruffly ordered the OPEC receptionist to get down on the floor, and then he had ripped out the telephone. Once on the floor the receptionist had tried to call for help, and another of the terrorists had shot at the entire telephone installation, destroying it. The woman was lucky that she had not been killed in the process. Mobile phones, now an everyday device and a standard tool in police raids, did not exist then. Of course, the police were using walkie-talkies, but it was still vital to be able to communicate by telephone.

Rawenduzy opened his medical bag. He was not looking for anything in particular. He felt a tension within that he could not get rid of. He felt he needed to do something useful. He checked his supplies. Syringes, various bandages, tampons, stethoscope – these and many other items were arranged neatly inside the bag.

What are you doing? Rawenduzy asked himself, surprised at his behavior. He never left his house without his medical bag, and his medical bag was always kept ready for emergencies. Why would it be different today?

Because everything was different today. Because you came here of your own free will, and now you are in the middle of an international terror drama. His inner voice spoke these words to him and advised him to be careful.

Finally. Liebhart, who had been speaking on the phone, put down the receiver and tried to appear calm. He did not succeed. In a muffled voice, he informed the leaders of the police force that Federal Chancellor Kreisky had returned to Vienna. Kreisky had gone to Lech am Arlberg to relax and to ski, but he had flown back to the capital as soon as he received the news of this frightful incident. He wanted to use his diplomatic connections in the Arab World, and if necessary to negotiate with the terrorists in person. He was determined to use every opportunity to avoid a bloodbath.

In addition, information had been leaked that the head of the terrorist group was the notorious "Carlos."

Carlos, Rawenduzy thought. "The Carlos?" Unintentionally he spoke the words aloud.

Liebhart glanced straight into the physician's eyes, his own eyes worried. Yes, his gaze communicated. The Carlos.

From the reports on the news, Rawenduzy knew that Carlos was Venezuelan. His real name was Illich Ramirez Sanchez, and he fought for the liberation of Palestinians, not always legally.

A dark figured hurried downstairs from the first floor. Rifles clicked as the police officers prepared to fire.

Abdesselam raised his arms. The terrorists had another demand. This time it absolutely had to be met. If not, they would shoot a hostage every fifteen minutes.

His voice trembled slightly as he explained further. Carlos, the boss, had issued a memorandum that was to be read on

Austrian radio stations every two hours. If this demand were not met, a hostage would be killed every fifteen minutes. In addition, the Algerian reported that the conference room where the hostages were held was covered in explosives and ignition cords. Should the SWAT team storm the building, the terrorists would blow up everything.

The terrorists called themselves "The Arm of the Arab Revolution". They were ready to die for the Palestinian cause.

During this discussion Rawenduzy again acted as the translator, since the oil minister was still excited and was mixing Arabic and French.

Carlos had also requested that the Ambassador of Libya, Al Ghadamsi, act as mediator between Carlos and the Austrian government.

When Abdesselam had finished there was a barrage of hectic telephone conversations. Rawenduzy addressed the Algerian personally. He, Rawenduzy, was a doctor with specialized medical training. He spoke Arabic, and could come to the conference room if desired to administer medical aid. The Algerian did not show any emotions, but promised to inform Carlos. The decision as to whether or not a physician was needed was entirely up to Carlos. He, Abdesselam, was in no position to comment. The Algerian turned his back on the startled doctor and climbed back up the stairs.

A short time later three OPEC employees came running into the entrance hall, calling loudly and imploringly, "DO NOT SHOOT!"

One of them handed over a six-page memo, written in French by Carlos. Carlos again demanded that his manifesto be read every two hours beginning at 6:00 PM on all radio stations. This was to continue on a regular basis.

Now the situation became dramatic. The only telephone was in constant use. The Federal Chancellery, The Ministry of the Interior, and the Special Police Force were contacted The circle was complete.

What alternatives did Kreisky have? As Chancellor of Austria, what decisions would he make? What decisions would he make as a human being? The terrorists had the richest hostages in the world at their mercy. Politics, power, and unimaginable sums of money were always tightly intertwined, but now the hostages were unprotected, exposed to the whims of terror.

Rawenduzy remembered his last personal meeting with Bruno Kreisky. He could still feel the charisma of the self-assured statesman. Nevertheless, he was happy not to be in Kreisky's position. Handling a crisis like this could mean sacrificing human lives. This must not happen. Kreisky and the authorities had to use every means at their disposal to avert such a catastrophe.

"He has to be found!" The harsh words were those of Dr. Nettel, the chief representative of the Austrian government. He had just arrived and he was speaking to the Section Chief, Dr. Danzinger, General Manager for Public Security.

Rawenduzy was jolted back to reality. What was going on?

The situation was extremely delicate. Libyan Ambassador Al Ghadamsi, the man the terrorists had demanded as a mediator, was not in Vienna. He was not even in Austria. This information, delivered by Danzinger to Nettel, was shattering.

What would happen now? Could they dare to propose another intermediary? Or would that make Carlos lose his nerves and start shooting hostages?

The precarious circumstances were underscored a moment later, when Abdesselam delivered a letter from one of the hostages, the Oil Minister of Saudi Arabia, Yamani. The letter was addressed to the Austrian Foreign Minister. Yamani begged that all of the terrorists' demands be met without exception. If the demands were not met, the hostages would pay for it with their lives.

Nettel and Danzinger instructed Abdesselam to inform the terror squad that Al Ghadamsi was not available. If there were another mediator acceptable to Carlos, they would ask that person to come immediately to OPEC Headquarters.

The reply came quickly. The alternative to Al Ghadamsi would be Al-Azawi.

Al-Azawi? Rihadh Al-Azawi! Al-Azawi was the Chargé d'Affaires of the Iraqi Embassy, and he was an old acquaintance of Rawenduzy. Rawenduzy knew him very well, and he doubted that this proud Iraqi would act as a negotiator in a terrorist attack. Nevertheless, Rawenduzy kept his thoughts to himself. The circumstances were not right for such comments. The Kurdish doctor would have to rely on the diplomatic skills of the Chargé d' Affaires if he chose to involve himself in the crisis.

Hectic telephone calls followed. Danzinger and Nettel hastily left the foyer and stepped into a police car.

Tension was mounting. What would happen if Al-Azawi could not be reached? Rawenduzy felt faint, and his pulse quickened. Why had he gotten involved? Why had he come here in the first place? To help. To help people. To be a physician, night and day. Was it his job? No, it was more than his job. It was his vocation, his mission. Often he had watched in wonder as his colleagues accepted patients' sick leave forms, filled them out without examining the patient, and billed the patients as usual. Sometimes the Hippocratic Oath seemed outdated. Sometimes he was amazed by his observations on these issues.

He shook his head slightly, took from his pocket a neatly folded handkerchief, and began cleaning his glasses to try to calm his nerves. For a moment, he closed his eyes, breathed deeply several times, and willed himself to stay in control.

"Good evening, Doctor!" The words came in Arabic, and without turning around Rawenduzy knew that the words were for him. The voice sounded so familiar. Almost relieved, he turned and greeted the newcomer.

"Brother Rihadh, so good to see you," the Kurd responded in Arabic.

At the request of the Austrian government, Al-Azawi had come to this place of horror to help free the hostages. Kreisky wanted to avoid bloodshed at any cost. He was ready for almost any reasonable concessions that were within his power.

Soon Nettel returned and he and Al-Azawi consulted with each other. Rawenduzy watched them both. The Chargé d'Affaires of the Iraqi Embassy was self-confident and calm. He wore a modern, sand-colored suit woven from exquisite wool. The suit was quite becoming and Al-Azawi presented an elegant appearance. His gaze was penetrating and seemed to take in everyone in the hall even while he was conducting a lively conversation with Nettel.

Time was pressing. Al-Azawi had to start his mission. Slowly, but with firm steps he ascended the steps to the conference room, the room that seemed to hold the answers to all problems. The people in the foyer held their breath.

What would the diplomat be able to accomplish? Would there be new demands? The police force was showing signs of fatigue, and grape juice and mineral water were being passed around. Rawenduzy refused the beverages; he had not eaten since his frugal breakfast, but he was neither hungry nor thirsty. He eagerly awaited the return of Al-Azawi. Perhaps a physician was needed on the first floor after all. If so, what would be waiting for him upstairs? If not, would it be because the terrorists were intentionally denying the hostages medical assistance?

Rawenduzy's thoughts were fixed on the people in that room, and on their distress. What would happen if the terrorists began to shoot people?

It was now past 6:00 PM, and the manifesto of the "Arm of the Arabic Revolution" was supposed to go on the air. However, the authorities had negotiated a short delay, until 6:20, which the terrorists agreed to, given the stipulation that the announcement still had to be re-broadcast within the prescribed two-hour period.

Fortunately, Carlos and his followers accepted the Iraqi diplomat as the mediator between themselves and the representatives of the Austrian government. Their first request was food and drink. All meals were to be without pork, for the terrorists were mostly Muslims. Carlos heatedly warned the Austrians not to play any dirty tricks, such as slipping sedatives into the food.

Had the OPEC Conference taken place as scheduled, the official dinner for the oil ministers would have taken place at the Hilton Hotel. Therefore, it was possible for food to be delivered swiftly to the OPEC Building, and soon this request was met.

For a while, in spite of the overall tension, nothing spectacular happened. The foyer of the building was still being guarded by heavily armed police officers, and talks continued at the highest diplomatic level to try to ensure a bloodless end to the drama.

Soon Al-Azawi passed on another of Carlos's demands. The terrorists were to be granted free conduct to the airport, and an airplane with pilot was to be put at their disposal. Carlos had also given instructions regarding the terrorist who had been severely injured in the early fighting, who was now in intensive care fighting for his life. Under no circumstances would he be left in Vienna. Furthermore, Carlos demanded that a bus be placed at their disposal at 7:00 AM at the latest. This bus would transport him, his companions, and the hostages to the airport.

Nettel and Danzinger were extremely disturbed. The terrorists' demands were becoming more and more brazen. Again, they raced to the Federal Chancellery. Kreisky had asked the representatives of the states whose oil ministers were being held in the OPEC building to join him, and he intended to use every possible international means to end the tragedy.

Vienna, the "Sleeping Beauty", had been rudely awakened from its political slumber. Suddenly, it had been thrust into the limelight of international attention. The entire world waited, breathlessly, to see how a neutral state like Austria would extract itself from this tragic dilemma without losing face or risking the loss of lives.

Al-Azawi was on his way back to the conference room. The Iraqi and the Kurd exchanged glances. They understood each other without saying a word. In the past, they had argued about politics many times, but now the situation was about saving lives, including perhaps their own.

Casually, Rawenduzy pointed to his dark medical bag. He asked the Iraqi mediator to talk to Carlos, and explain to him that a doctor was available who could administer immediate medical assistance to the hostages if need be. The diplomat nodded absently. He was preoccupied with Kreisky and the terrorists' ultimatum. He knew that his life could be in danger should the Chancellor choose a radical solution to the problem, a solution without regard for the lives of the people involved. However, the idea of having a SWAT team storm the conference room had already been discussed and dismissed because laced throughout the room there were ignition cords wired to explosives.

Al-Azawi knew that these criminals would never surrender, and would spare no lives, including their own. They were following orders. They had committed murder on orders, and on orders they had permanently jettisoned their morality and conscience.

Time ticked away mercilessly. Carlos's memorandum was read regularly on the radio. The terrorists heard it on the system they had been given and acknowledged that they had found it acceptable, and that their first demand had been met.

Danzinger and Nettel had been instructed to satisfy the terrorists' additional demands as quickly and unbureaucratically as possible. They were easily able to organize an Austrian

Postal Services bus to wait in front of the OPEC building at the appointed time. Furthermore, two Austrian Airlines pilots had volunteered to participate in the effort to free the hostages. They would fly an airplane under the terrorists' direction. No one knew the destination yet, so no one could put together a flight plan or a weather prognosis, both of which were normally considered essential. Everyone would have to rely on the pilots' training and experience.

However, one problem remained. They had not figured out how to transport the wounded terrorist, who was still in intensive care in the hospital. The Austrian intermediaries informed Carlos that their comrade was likely to die during the journey. Carlos's cold reply brought negotiations to a screeching halt:

"He will fly. Dead or alive."

Dr. Steinbereithner, Chief Surgeon of the Intensive Care Unit at the hospital, conducted long, heated discussions with two representatives of the Austrian government, insisting that as a physician he absolutely would not take responsibility for releasing the terrorist. In his opinion, this would mean the patient's certain death. Politics meant nothing to Dr. Steinbereithner – they were discussing a human life. As a physician it was not his job to decide between right and wrong; his concern was keeping this half-dead man alive. He felt everyone had a right to live, and he would not deny this man that right no matter what the political cost.

Without a doubt, Dr. Steinbereithner displayed morals of the highest quality, as well as admirable medical ethics. However, the hostages' lives were also at stake; their lives had to be protected as well. Carlos had been adamant about the issue of the wounded terrorist, and had left no doubt that he would proceed with a massacre if his demands were not met.

There were more frantic telephone calls. Was there no way out? What would happen next? It was suggested that a physician be found to accompany the wounded man, and this suggestion seemed both logical and plausible to Dr. Steinbereithner. Moreover, Carlos accepted the proposal and agreed that if the terrorist died in transport the attending physician would not be held responsible for it. Feverishly the authorities began to search for a doctor who would be capable of withstanding the tremendous pressure of the situation while at the same time administering competent medical treatment.

It was already past midnight, and all of the problems seemed to have been solved, so Rawenduzy decided to go home. His presence, it seemed, was no longer necessary, since Al-Azawi had passed on a message from Carlos that a doctor was neither needed nor desired. Rawenduzy felt rather tired. Since he had arrived on the scene there had been non-stop tension, and Rawenduzy had eaten absolutely nothing. All of this was beginning to take its toll. Now that the Rescue Society of Vienna had sent sufficient medical staff to the OPEC Headquarters, it was clear that the Kurdish doctor was no longer needed.

With a jerk, he lifted his black medical supply bag from the shabby chair in the porter's office. The chair, now free of the unwanted load, groaned loudly and then fell silent. Rawenduzy sighted Liebhart and approached him to say goodbye. The Chief of Operations, somewhat surprised, shook Rawenduzy's hand and asked him to stay. Rawenduzy put the medical bag back on the creaky chair, and quickly picked up the phone and dialed his home to tell his wife where he was. For a few seconds he allowed his thoughts to wander to his two young sons. They would be sleeping peacefully in their cozy beds, protected, secure, and in dreamland.

Abruptly the voice of Ambassador Nettel brought Rawenduzy back to the brutal reality of the entrance hall.

"Dr. Rawenduzy, may we be completely frank with you?"

Next to Nettel stood Danzinger. He cleared his throat and seemed to take note of Rawenduzy's penetrating glance.

"Our Chancellor has a question that only you can answer," Nettel continued. Danzinger cleared his throat again.

"Kreisky would like to know if you would be willing to accompany the injured terrorist on the flight and attend to him medically. The destination of the flight is unknown."

Now it was out in the open. Both representatives looked nervous. Hopes of liberating the hostages were hanging on a thread, and tension was mounting.

Thoughts raced through Rawenduzy's head. Who? Kreisky himself. Of course. The promise. He remembered precisely. But that had been more than a year ago, at the blood bank. I am at your disposal, Rawenduzy had said.

Soon, after observing the race in his head for a long moment, Rawenduzy knew which side had won.

"Yes," he said. "I will do it. Tell the Chancellor he can count on me. However, I would like to point out that I am a specialist in internal medicine, not a surgeon. Nevertheless, I will take on the risk that the patient may not be able to endure the strain of transport and that he could die."

Rawenduzy heard himself speak as if he were listening to another person. He sounded cool and composed. Only those who knew him well could have read from his nostrils how he really felt.

"Do you know what you are getting into?" Nettel said. He had raised his voice and seemed to have completely forgotten to act as an Ambassador. Apparently, he had been seized with sympathy for the likeable Kurd.

"Yes. I do," Rawenduzy replied. "I will go. Please inform Dr. Kreisky."

Nothing could shake Rawenduzy – he had been learning self-control since childhood.

Nettel shook his head. Danzinger, who had witnessed the entire conversation, looked at Rawenduzy as if mesmerized and began to chew nervously on his lip. He remained silent. Comments seemed superfluous, and he was on duty, not in a psychological counseling session.

Ambassador Nettel took both of Rawenduzy's hands and expressed deep gratitude. Danzinger followed suit. It was a brief but touching show of humanity.

The Chancellor was informed of Rawenduzy's answer. Again time passed, and all waited, and Rawenduzy had a chance to ponder the magnitude of his decision. Strangely, he was not afraid. He focused his mind and began to think through all of the medical scenarios that could unfold. He decided he had to discuss the case in detail with Dr. Steinbereithner. This might give the wounded terrorist, not to mention himself, a chance to survive. No matter what they had promised, it was anyone's guess as to how the terrorists would react should their comrade die.

It was very early Monday morning, close to 4:00 AM. Nettel and Danzinger, who had hurried off to the Chancellery after Rawenduzy's decision, returned. Danzinger was the first to address Rawenduzy. Dr. Steinbereithner had been consulted, and he had provided instructions for further procedures. All necessary steps and precautions had been taken. They were only waiting for Rawenduzy.

Both representatives of the Austrian government wished the brave physician the best of luck.

This was only the beginning of a very dangerous undertaking.

Insha-Allah, thought Rawenduzy in Arabic. With the will of God.

The Terrorist's Physician

Night had long since fallen over the city. Vienna slept its dreamless sleep, buried in a chilly darkness and exposed to the bitter cold. Pale streetlights cast eerie shadows on the snow-covered road. Along the streets hurried solitary figures wrapped in heavy clothing, and once in a while a car glided through the streets.

It was Monday morning at about 4:30 AM, only two days before Christmas.

Rawenduzy rubbed his eyes. The traffic light in front of him was red, and he was exhausted. He had not slept well the night before. Luckily, his tension had eased a bit in the familiar surroundings of his car. He stretched out as far as he could in the driver's seat. His thoughts were already fixed on the intensive unit at the city hospital.

Green. The traffic light glared almost menacingly. The lonely driver shifted the car into first gear and edged it cautiously forward. Rawenduzy told himself to pay attention. Turn right at the next street, then straight ahead, again to the right, and then left along the street.

Finally. Finally he could see the colossal hospital building. But what was this? He could not believe his eyes. The city hospital looked like a fortress. A police squad had sealed off the entire building. Rawenduzy tried to navigate through the crowd.

"What do you want here?" The voice of the police officer was harsh and bitter. "You can't come in. Turn around and drive back, and quickly!"

This was all Rawenduzy needed. He did not feel like arguing, and he began to get annoyed. Because of his past, he hated confrontations with police officers, even if they were only verbal confrontations. He forced himself to remain under control.

"I am Dr. Rawenduzy and I have come to pick up the wounded terrorist from intensive care," he said. He let his eyes shut slightly and added under his breath, "If it is OK with you."

The police officer changed his attitude immediately, apologized, and allowed Rawenduzy to pass. Rawenduzy parked his Volvo in the space reserved for the head of the clinic, and was politely greeted by a plainclothes police officer. Rawenduzy told him that the Volvo was his own car, and that in the event that he should not return he would appreciate it if someone could tell his wife where it was parked.

The officer stared at Rawenduzy in disbelief. What kind of a person was this man? He was thinking about his car in a situation like this? The police officer was used to people acting coolly and showing nerves of steel, but this doctor was amazing. This man had volunteered of his own free will to accompany the wounded terrorist on his flight into the unknown.

The plainclothes officer alerted the police force that the doctor had arrived.

So this was how a hero looked, thought the plainclothes officer. Or was he just an adventurer, a normal person out for thrills? What in the world had made this friendly and apparently normal middle-aged man agree to this? With a mixture of admiration and regret, the officer watched as the doctor locked his car and vanished into the hospital.

Watching the Kurd disappear, the police officer was happy that he was a plainclothes officer. He had only to be on duty there at the hospital, and if all went well in a few hours he would be safe in bed in his warm apartment. He pulled his cap down further over his face and put his hands over his ears. They were cold and they hurt.

Rawenduzy walked quickly down the brightly lit corridor. The door to one of the operating rooms was ajar. Strange, he thought. Out of the corner of his eye, he took note of the operating table, the monitors, the anesthetic equipment, and the respirator. Normally the operating room was locked when no one was using it.

At the end of the corridor, a door opened. Through the door stepped two physicians, talking quietly to each other. They saw Rawenduzy and stopped abruptly.

"Good morning," said Rawenduzy. "Here I am."

Dr. Steinbereithner did not greet Rawenduzy back. The Austrian doctor was visibly annoyed.

"Are you tired of life, Doctor?" he said. "This man is seriously injured. He may very well die. Just what are you thinking? I would really like to know."

He continued in this way, and after a few minutes, Rawenduzy had lost patience with him. This was the last thing he needed. He had no interest in listening to annoying questions while the answers to those questions were still up in the air. He had already decided to accompany the patient, no matter what happened. He interrupted Dr. Steinbereithner brusquely.

"I am fully aware of the situation, Professor," he said. "We are, however, not dealing only with a medical problem. This is also a matter of politics. Should the patient die, Carlos is responsible, not the doctors."

The head of intensive care was not used to being disputed, especially not publicly, and from then on there was a dead silence between Steinbereithner and the Kurdish doctor.

Dr. Sporn, the second physician of intensive care, had stayed in the background during this exchange. The plans called for him to go to the airport with Rawenduzy to assist if need be. Rawenduzy requested a doctor's uniform – he did not have his own with him – and, correct as always, promised to return it after the mission. Provided he returned from the mission, he added.

The head nurse complied with his request with a bemused smile, and soon Rawenduzy was pulling on a white doctor's jacket bearing the logo of the city hospital.

The three physicians retired to a consultation room to discuss further medical details. The patient had just come out of surgery, and his condition was critical. The hospital staff had readied blood transfusions, Ringers solutions, sugar solutions, and various other medicines to keep the patient alive and guarantee oxygen supply. Drainage tubes had been inserted into his abdomen, a procedure that was essential to the patient's survival. Furthermore, a catheter now ran from the patient's bladder, a logical measure in a case like this.

Steinbereithner again pointed out the great risk in transporting the patient, and the possible lethal consequences that could result. He handed the terrorist's medical report to Rawenduzy without comment, and with a curt "Good luck," he disappeared.

Sporn, who had remained silent throughout the entire confrontation, expressed his full admiration for Rawenduzy and offered to fly with him if needed. Rawenduzy thanked him but refused the offer. He could not make such a decision without the approval of Carlos. This would be far too dangerous, and Rawenduzy would not jeopardize the life of his young colleague.

Rawenduzy used the next moment to call his wife and inform her of his decision. She had been listening to the radio and had already heard the news. A monologue followed, full of concern and worry that made dialogue impossible.

From the moment Rawenduzy had entered the hospital the corridor had been filled with a low murmur, and now the murmur became louder. The nurses, with the approval of the Head of Intensive Care, had prepared the "somewhat unique" patient for transport. Plainclothes officers and heavily armed police troops had secured the hallways from the sick room to the building's exit. Outside, two ambulances and a police escort stood ready.

Both doctors followed the stretcher with the wounded terrorist. When they exited the building, Rawenduzy saw that there were two ambulances, and was taken aback. The hospital authorities informed him that the second ambulance was a spare, and would be brought along in case of unforeseen circumstances. Nothing was to be left to chance. In case the first ambulance broke down or malfunctioned somehow, the second ambulance would allow the operation to proceed without interruption.

The objective was to transport the wounded terrorist to the Vienna airport and to put him on the plane as quickly as possible.

Soon the doors of the dark green ambulance were shut tightly with Rawenduzy and the terrorist inside. The patient was moaning, and sweat covered his brow. His dark hair seemed plastered to his forehead. Rawenduzy looked at the face of the pale young man, and suddenly he could not understand terrorism. How vulnerable each human being was, how helpless when the body becomes one's enemy rather than one's friend. One's mortal enemy. Here before him the flame of life slowly ebbed away, yet Rawenduzy could see that the will to live was unbroken.

The man groaned again, interrupting the doctor's train of thought. The man pointed to his abdomen, which was covered by a blanket.

"Pain," he whispered.

Outside frost had covered the streets, and it was making the ambulance ride uncomfortable. Each bump was hurting the patient.

Pain. Pain. The man's eyes were wide open. He closed them and whimpered softly. Rawenduzy slipped the rubber band of a sphygmomanometer, an instrument that measures blood pressure, onto the terrorist's arm, activated the balloon, and took hold of his stethoscope. A catheter had been inserted into the man's arm near his elbow. Rawenduzy wanted to inject an analgesic to counter the pain, and he decided to do it through the catheter to make it easier on the terrorist. This done, he knocked on the forward window of the ambulance and motioned for the driver to reduce speed drastically. Soon the ambulance had slowed to a crawl.

Repeatedly the physician checked the oxygen supply. He also tried to strike up a conversation. He introduced himself and attempted, in several languages, to explain his presence at the young man's side. However, his attempts to communicate seemed unsuccessful. The young man did not respond to any language, be it German, English, or even Arabic.

Was this the face of a brutal killer? Rawenduzy could not believe it, but his common sense remembered all too well the details of the terrorist attack. Nevertheless, Rawenduzy was a physician, and that meant he was an ally of life and had a responsibility to fight to keep death at bay.

"Water!" whispered the patient.

Rawenduzy was still thinking about the events at the OPEC building. He looked up as the patient whispered again.

"Water!"

The man's lips were parched and his mouth was dry and he was looking fearfully at Rawenduzy. The doctor knew he could not quench the wounded man's thirst. Under no circumstances could a newly post-operative patient be given liquid – it would kill him.

Rawenduzy moistened a piece of gauze and applied it gently to the patient's lips. He did this several times until he felt the patient begin to relax. Nevertheless, Rawenduzy sensed a piercing anxiety within this defenseless man. It would be so much easier if they could speak to each other.

Perhaps he thinks I am from the police, Rawenduzy thought. If that were the case, the patient would probably not even want to appear to understand him. Rawenduzy decided to attempt to win the confidence of this helpless man, who was now completely at Rawenduzy's mercy.

Rawenduzy searched his pockets and pulled out a small, non-descript booklet similar to a driver's license. It was his physician's license – black letters printed on gray paper. Rawenduzy opened it slowly and showed the man his photograph. Again, he tried in several languages to explain that he was a doctor of internal medicine, and that he was there only to take care of the young man. Yet the severely injured terrorist seemed to understand nothing. His pale face showed pain and distrust. Rawenduzy decided to face reality, and he slipped his ID back into his coat pocket.

What a pity, he said to himself. He checked the bottle containing the infusion. Everything was under control. The Ringer's solution was dripping at the prescribed rate.

The wounded man had opened his eyes slightly, but was avoiding eye contact with the doctor. Rawenduzy looked out of the window to try to determine their location. To the left of the road he spotted the Schwechat oil refinery. It was lit up by countless bright lights. Behind them drove the second ambulance and behind it the rear portion of the police escort. The vehicles' blue emergency lights cast demonic shadows over the countryside.

"Water!" Automatically Rawenduzy touched the lips of his patient with the moist gauze.

He needed to check the blood pressure again. Could the wounded man have developed a fever? Could that be why he was so thirsty? A few minutes later Rawenduzy breathed a sigh of relief. Everything was as it should be. There was no abnormal temperature, no abnormal pulse. The man was unstable, but the chances he would make it to the airplane alive were good.

Rawenduzy wondered if the medical equipment would work properly at high altitudes. He hoped the changes in air pressure would not affect the dripping of the infusions. In addition, he had to make sure the passengers did not smoke – an oxygen bottle plus a burning cigarette could equal instant death to all. Suddenly he wanted to speak to a specialist. He realized he had questions about air pressure and medical equipment that he could not answer by himself because he had never dealt with such things.

The ambulance driver slowed down. In front of the ambulance, the police cars had already turned into the airport. There were heavily armed police squads everywhere. The atmosphere in airports is normally hectic, but today at the Vienna airport all was ghostly silent. The terminals were barely lit, and the taxi stands were empty.

Soon the police vehicles ahead had been joined by a pilot car, which bore on its back a sign with the words "Follow Me" and drove ahead of the police cars. Behind the police followed the two ambulances, and behind them more police cars. Soon the convoy had reached the tarmac. They passed the freight area, then the main halls, then the administrative buildings, and finally the brightly lit airport tower.

Rawenduzy checked the patient, and then checked the patient's breathing device. He had to make sure that the patient had an uninterrupted oxygen supply. The sick man moaned again faintly and pointed to his abdomen.

"Pain," he whispered.

The physician activated the sphygmomanometer and discovered alarmingly low readings. He immediately injected medicine to stabilize the patient's circulation.

The convoy seemed to have reached its destination. The ambulance stopped, and its doors were opened. Bitter cold air pushed its way into the cabin. Outside there were police officers and paramedics. Behind them Rawenduzy could see the open tail of a jet airplane. A collapsible staircase had been lowered, allowing entrance to the passenger area.

Dr. Sporn, who had followed in the second ambulance, appeared at the door of the first ambulance. He examined the wounded man and again offered his assistance to Rawenduzy. Rawenduzy accepted his help in transporting the patient from the ambulance into the airplane. They would

Vienna Schwechat Airport. December 22, 1975

"The Goodbye": Interior Minister Rösch bids farewell to the terrorist Carlos.

need to exercise extreme caution when they handled the infusion container and the oxygen bottle.

The patient was quickly wrapped in an additional blanket. The doctors gave instructions to the paramedics as to how to transport the patient, and two of the medics carefully lifted the stretcher from the ambulance. Outside, police officers took position, their rifles readied in firing position.

The quiet of morning was interrupted by loud, encoded messages from the police radios. Everything had to be done quickly. Rawenduzy followed the stretcher.

Suddenly it struck him that he had no passport. He had no passport? In a situation like this, how could he even think of something so trivial? He did not even know their destination, and it could very well be a one-way trip. Why on earth would he need a passport?

Annoyed with himself he took measure of the inside of the airplane. The authorities had shifted three rows to provide a raised space for the stretcher. However, this would mean that the physician would have to stand to treat the patient.

Sporn checked the oxygen supply and made sure that the infusion was working. The plane seemed to be adequately heated, but Rawenduzy elected to keep the extra blanket on the wounded man to keep him warm.

"Should I not come along?" Sporn asked. He had registered the concerned look on his colleague's face as Rawenduzy monitored the patient's circulation and tried to ease his pain with intravenous injections. In the course of the trip, Rawenduzy had many times abandoned hope of keeping the man alive, only to have his hope revived again. The terrorist's condition was extremely unstable.

Rawenduzy declined Sporn's offer. He did not want to expose him to danger, and would not allow him on a trip with a one-way ticket, a ticket no one had bought to begin with.

Sporn wished the Kurdish doctor the world's best and took his leave. Rawenduzy promised to meet for a cup of tea very soon. Sporn was touched, and without looking back, he hurried down the stairway of the DC-9 jet.

May God bless him, Sporn thought. He was consumed with worry for this unselfish Kurd. On the runway, a police vehicle waited for him. He opened the door and got in.

The clock struck 8:00 AM.

Inside the plane, Rawenduzy was absorbed in the care of his patient. Occasionally he risked a short glance through the side windows or the rear entrance of the aircraft. Suddenly a well-dressed man came up the stairs. He smiled and offered Rawenduzy his hand. His voice was friendly.

"I am Carlos," he said.

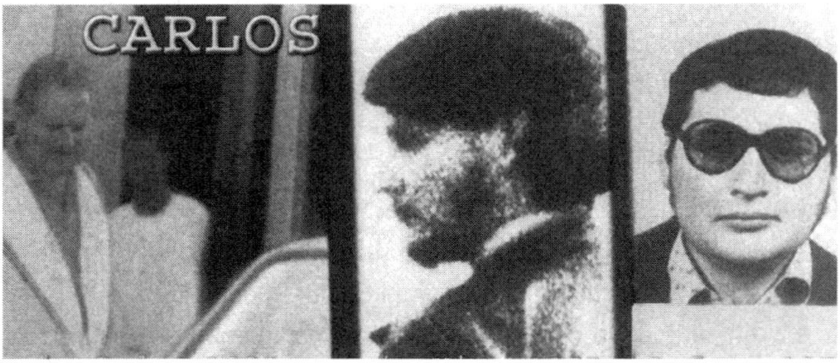

His glance was cool, his mouth sensual. His outfit resembled that of a playboy rather than the leader of a band of killers. Professionally, one would sooner think him a loose-living trust fund baby than a terrorist. He looked like a bad boy actor in a third rate thriller who was trying to make his role stand out with a spectacular entrance.

This was Carlos, the famous macho man and darling of women. This was Carlos, the rising star of international crime. Carlos, he of the limitless horizon. Illich Ramirez Sanchez, aka Carlos. The Jackal.

Rawenduzy could hardly mask his surprise. Before he could say anything, Carlos thanked him for agreeing to care for the wounded man.

"They tell me you are from Iraq?" Carlos said. His question was worded in proper English and was delivered in a friendly tone, and something about all this yanked Rawenduzy back to reality and to the danger of the situation.

"No," he replied curtly. Why should he give further details? He was a physician and his private life was nobody's business.

The terrorist frowned and seemed a bit annoyed.

Rawenduzy explained that he was from Iraqi Kurdistan, and hence was a Kurd, not an Iraqi. To be exact he was a Kurdish physician, and consequently not at all an Arab.

Carlos's face relaxed. He laughed and replied, this time in Arabic, "Oh yes! The Kurdish problem!"

They exchanged a bit of small talk, and Carlos turned to the injured man, stroked his sweaty hair, and whispered something into his ear. Rawenduzy observed the scene and wondered what was going on. What was Carlos up to? This loving gesture did not fit with the image of the deadly things these men had done.

"The patient's condition is critical," Rawenduzy said. He did not want to disturb Carlos, but he felt he had to be completely honest about the wounded man's state. Above all, he had to make sure that the leader of the terrorists was fully informed of the situation.

Why was this sick man not left in the hospital, Rawenduzy questioned the terrorist leader? He could die during the flight. As a physician, Rawenduzy would not take responsibility for this. If the man died, it would be Carlos's fault. Rawenduzy was tormented by uncertainty and deeply concerned for the patient, and as the future was unpredictable he felt he had to express his thoughts and feelings openly.

Carlos took his accusations in stride. He put his hand on the doctor's shoulder and said simply:

"I have orders to take him with us under any circumstances – dead or alive."

Rawenduzy realized there was no room here for an ethical discussion. In the world of evil, the individual did not count, and it was only in isolated cases that a lost individual was missed. What was important was only the whole, the group, the cause, and it was not to be challenged under any circumstances.

Somewhat delicately, Rawenduzy said that Carlos would have to make sure that no one smoked on the aircraft. The doctor gestured to the oxygen bottles that were so vital to the survival of the patient. A burning cigarette could turn this life-sustaining machine into a bomb.

And how long would it take, he thought? A fraction of a second. The authorities and the official reports would say that a shoot-out or an explosive attack was responsible for the airplane's crash.

And survivors? None, Rawenduzy thought.

Where was the plane's destination, Rawenduzy asked. Most importantly, when would they land there? Rawenduzy tried to impress on "The Jackal" that the supply of oxygen in the bottles was limited.

The terrorist shrugged his shoulders and promised to inform Rawenduzy in due time, and he disappeared into the interior of the jet. Rawenduzy was taken aback and let his eyes follow the terrorist leader.

What was he doing now? Rawenduzy wondered as he watched Carlos. No. This just could not be true.

Carlos was systematically searching the passenger area – each nook and cranny, behind each curtain. Time was of the essence and the head of the terrorist group appeared to be taking all the time in the world. He was examining absolutely everything.

"Water! Please! Water!" The injured man had opened his eyes and was begging for a drink. He seemed the thirst disturbed him more than the pain.

Rawenduzy moistened the man's parched lips several times. He tried to explain soothingly that he could not give the young man water to drink because drinking liquid would endanger his life. He spoke first in German and then in English. The features of the young man relaxed somewhat, and Rawenduzy had the strong feeling that the man understood him. Yet he remained silent, rolling his eyes and showing no reaction.

Very odd, thought Rawenduzy.

Carlos had finally finished his search and now he headed for the entrance. Looking out, he gestured briefly with his left hand and two of his comrades, heavily armed, came onto the plane.

Silently, the hostages, eleven oil ministers, climbed up the steps and into the plane. Their faces were pale and tense and their expressions registered the full impact of this diabolical affair.

In the rear of the group came two additional armed terrorists. One of them was a rather small woman. She was well dressed in a long skirt of the high fashion of those days. She held in her hands a deadly weapon. Her eyes were deep-set brown, almost black, and her gaze was piercing and without emotion. She looked more like a wild animal than a kind-hearted woman. She did not fit Rawenduzy's image of womanhood in the least.

When she passed Rawenduzy, he felt nervous. She ignored him and went straight to the sickbed. She bent over the wounded man and looked at him, her black hair falling partly over the young man's face, and, barely audibly, she whispered into his ear. The wounded terrorist seemed grateful, almost happy, and tried to express his feelings by turning his head slightly.

After a few minutes, he closed his eyes again. A stabbing pain seemed to wrack his body.

"Pain!" he cried. The young woman stepped aside and turned toward the passenger area without batting an eyelid. She held her weapon tightly and proceeded into the cockpit.

Rawenduzy checked the patient's infusion and injected a painkiller, and soon the patient had fallen asleep. A terrorist sat down next to the doctor and the patient. He had released the safety catch of his submachine gun. Rawenduzy thought he looked Arab.

Carlos was pacing up and down the center aisle. He was the only one in the group without a gun.

Shortly before 9:00AM Carlos hurried down the isle to the gangway. Through a window, Rawenduzy could see Otto Rösch, acting Austrian Minister of the Interior, standing on the runway. Rawenduzy decided to step out quickly to take his leave of the government's officials. The Arab guarding the wounded man took no notice of him.

Rösch thanked Rawenduzy for volunteering to help. He said the doctor had contributed towards the first step of the drama's solution.

They exchanged a few additional remarks, and Rawenduzy was back on the plane. He had to keep this patient alive. His death would cause more problems than Rawenduzy could imagine. Rawenduzy had realized that the patient's survival had become a bit of a bargaining chip, a bargaining chip that could help insure his own survival and that of the hostages. The wounded man was something the terrorists had to protect, and if the wounded terrorist survived everyone's chances of leaving the plane alive and returning to safety would increase. That made Rawenduzy and his opinions important.

Carlos shook hands with Minister Rösch and dashed back onto the plane.

This, the handshake, turned out to be a giant mistake on the part of Rösch. The next day there appeared eye-catching headlines about the handshake in both the Austrian and international newspapers. It was a frightful faux pas by the Minister of the Interior, an everlasting blunder from a political as well as a human standpoint, and it ended up humiliating Austria and her citizens.

Apparently, the two Austrian Airlines pilots were already in the cockpit. All of the plane's doors were shut, and the plane began to move slowly from the airfield, across Vorfeldstrasse, and onto the taxiway. The pilots stopped and sent the standard message to the tower: Ready for take-off.

Under the circumstances the message was, of course, silly. Because of the hostage crisis, the airport and all of the airspace nearby had been closed to all air traffic. The tower could have given them permission to take off at any time.

The pilots ran through their technical checks according to their normal routine. The captain, Ing. Manfred Pollak, and his co-pilot Otto Herald took a deep breath. Their friends in the tower wished them "a nice trip", and said they hoped they saw each other again. The two pilots had volunteered for this mission, just like Rawenduzy.

Pollack felt the vibrations of the great bird as it ascended. In one way everything was going according to routine, yet today everything was different. They were highly experienced aviators and the weather conditions were stable. The only weakness was in the interior of the plane, with the passengers.

Destination, Baghdad, Pollack had been told. The post take-off procedures had been completed, and the DC-9 was cruising towards an uncertain fate.

Back in the plane, Rawenduzy's job had become difficult. Despite the pressurized cabin, the infusion had stopped dripping, even though the tube was completely clear. Now what was wrong?

He quickly transferred the solution to a syringe and injected it directly through the catheter inserted into the terrorist's vein. He periodically checked the patient's blood pressure and pulse, and kept an eye on the oxygen supply. At regular intervals, he administered circulatory stimulants and painkillers.

Next to the Arab guard, there were several medium-sized wooden boxes. Rawenduzy wondered what else the killers could possibly have in store for them. Could the boxes contain ammunition and explosives? Hand grenades?

The Arab looked at Rawenduzy as if he could read his mind, but he remained silent. Suddenly Rawenduzy heard himself say in Arabic:

"Why did you kill three people?"

The man was startled. He began to explain, almost guiltily. They had strict orders only to use their weapons in critical situations, but if they had not used their guns, they would have been arrested and their plan would have failed.

Jussuf, as the Arab was called, fell silent. The woman terrorist, Nada, had come to the back of the plane. She leaned over the wounded man again and began to whisper into his ear.

Rawenduzy could not understand what she was saying, and he became angry. He could not even recognize the language they were using.

Nada looked up and addressed the physician in perfect English. "Are you hungry or thirsty?"

Rawenduzy asked for a glass of orange juice.

Nada brought him some orange juice, the frosty expression never leaving her face. Somewhere ahead in the airplane Rawenduzy could hear Carlos arguing loudly with the oil minister of Algeria. Some of the hostages had also entered the conversation. Intermittently, Carlos disappeared into the cockpit or came to the rear of the aircraft to visit his injured comrade.

More than an hour of flying time had elapsed. The plan was flying somewhere above the Mediterranean Sea. Rawenduzy approached Carlos and asked him for the destination.

Evasively, Carlos murmured something about Baghdad.

Baghdad? Had Rawenduzy heard correctly? Baghdad? No. He would never fly to Baghdad. His eyes flared up with rage, and he was gripped by a cold fury.

"The oxygen will last for a half an hour, or an hour at most!" he blistered at Carlos. "By that time we will have to have landed somewhere. Do you want to watch your friend die, or would you like him to survive? The decision is in your hands."

He was speaking sarcastically and Carlos could not possibly miss it. However, the terrorist remained calm, only his pressed lips registering signs of annoyance. He promised Rawenduzy that he would make a decision and inform the doctor accordingly.

Precious time was being wasted, and nothing was happening. The dial on the oxygen container had almost fallen to zero. In desperation, Rawenduzy plucked up his courage and marched directly through the plane, all the way forward to the cockpit. He introduced himself to the pilots inside, and asked politely for the position of the jet. Pollak explained that they were flying over the coast of North Africa.

Rawenduzy left the cockpit and made his way through the central isle to the back of the plane. He stopped in the area where the hostages were being held and inquired as to whether they needed medical attention. Most of them were completely exhausted and had their eyes closed. The rest were too afraid to speak.

Rawenduzy looked at the terrorists who guarded them. They were armed to the teeth, and sitting next to them the hostages did indeed look doomed. Amougazar, the Iranian oil minister, bent forward. Rawenduzy thought he wanted to tell him something, and asked him how the minister was doing.

"You can see for yourself!" the oil minister answered briskly. His eyes turned towards the sky. "We are all sitting in the same boat!"

Rawenduzy wanted to reply, but he did not. Iran. The thought of Iran filled him with pain. Recently, in May, the Shah of Iran had signed a peace treaty with Saddam Hussein, the Iraqi dictator. Consequences for the rebellious Kurds had been dramatic. This was contemporary history, it was hopelessly unjust, and at this moment for some reason, it hit home. The events of that time seemed to bring up the question as to which of the international superpowers had done anything for the Kurds other than provide lip service.

He returned to the back and checked the blood pressure of his patient. There was nothing to worry about. The young man requested water repeatedly, and each time Rawenduzy moistened his lips. Nearby Jussuf stood, firm and silent, looking down the center isle or observing his moaning comrade.

Rawenduzy wondered what was going on in the head of this young Arab. What could have happened to him to make him join a group of terrorists? What wicked role was he playing in this mission?

What a pity, thought Rawenduzy. At first glance, he is a human being, just like me. However, he has followed orders until he has developed into a brute, blind to humanity, guided by unconditional, self-destructive obedience.

The oxygen supply had dwindled to the absolute minimum. Rawenduzy could just about no longer feel his body. He was completely drained. Sweat had accumulated on his brow and he continued as if he were a machine. Take blood pressure. Give infusions. Inject air into the receptacle. Check the pulse. And on, and on, and on... and constantly worry that a tear in the sutures from the surgery would cause the patient to bleed to death.

"Doctor, we will soon land in Algiers," said a voice. Carlos had entered unnoticed.

What had Rawenduzy just heard? They were landing in Algiers? When?

In about twenty minutes, Carlos replied.

Rawenduzy could not believe his ears. They would make it. The injured man would survive. Allah be praised.

He took a piece of gauze and dried his brow. He gestured to Jussuf and said he had to speak to the pilot, and that it was urgent. As soon as they landed, the patient needed immediate medical assistance at the airport.

Yes. We are landing, he thought. An end to the drama had come within reach. This was wonderful. It is true that I volunteered for this, and now that it is over, I am overjoyed.

Rawenduzy was hurrying down the center aisle to the cockpit, relief taking possession of him. In the cockpit, Pollak and Herold had already begun their landing maneuvers. The physician asked them to radio instructions to the tower at Algiers. The authorities at Algiers must make sure that when the plane landed there was an oxygen container present, as well as an ambulance to transport the severely wounded patient. Of course there must be medical staff.

Rawenduzy carefully closed the door to the cockpit and glanced at his watch. It was shortly before noon. He wondered if his two young sons had had their lunch yet. What might they have had? Had they noticed that their father had not come home?

No, he had not been on an excursion today. He had been doing his duty. Duty? Yes, indeed, it had been duty, and he had done it voluntarily. Nevertheless, how would he be able to explain terrorism, Kreisky, and his own involvement in these events to his innocent children?

However, it was not over yet, he thought. He returned to his patient. He began running through his checkups again. Jussuf only nodded to him. The Arab still had his finger on the trigger of the submachine gun.

The sick man had his eyes closed, and his face even seemed relaxed. His accomplice, who had been checking on him in short but regular intervals, must have told him of the pending landing.

Rawenduzy glanced out the window. The aircraft was already descending, and Algiers lay peacefully below them.

Listen. What was that strange noise? Ah. It was just the landing gear making such a racket.

The pilot took the jet into a steep, leftward curve, then straight on, and then to the left again. The surface of the earth came closer. One could almost touch the palm trees.

Then the Austrian Airlines DC-9 had safely landed, and it was rolling slowly towards the airport complex.

Rawenduzy swallowed to ease the pressure in his ears. For the last time he moistened the parched lips of his patient. The patient, however, did not thank him, but kept his eyes fixed on the ceiling.

The airplane had come to a standstill. Soon the back door opened and physicians and nurses came up the gangway. Carlos greeted them and referred them to the Kurdish physician. Rawenduzy and the medical staff exchanged some friendly words, as if among everyday colleagues, and then Rawenduzy handed over the medical report that Dr. Steinbereithner had compiled prior to departure. With utmost care, the patient was lifted out of the jet.

He is alive. Thank goodness, he is alive, thought Rawenduzy. He followed the rescue squad with his eyes and breathed a sigh of relief.

He had done his duty. As a physician, he had done his duty. As an Austrian from Kurdistan, he had done his duty. Exhausted yet delighted, he secretly admitted to himself that after so many years of medical training he had just now put the finishing touches on his specialized medical training, and this at an altitude of 10,000 meters.

Carlos (center) with the Algerian Oil Minister (right)
after landing in Algiers. December 22, 1975.

Between Heaven and Heroism

And suddenly you realize:
It is time to start something new,
and to trust in the magic of its beginning.
Meister Eckhart

The orange juice was cool and tasted like ambrosia in his mouth. Delicious. Rawenduzy closed his eyes and tried to relax. Free. Finally free. World, I want to embrace you. Life can be so very beautiful.

He was reclining comfortably on a seat in the VIP lounge of the Algiers Airport, savoring the delightful juice. Had he dreamt all of this? Had he just awakened? He simply could not fathom it all – a terror attack in Vienna, and he right in the middle of it.

Vienna. It seemed like an eternity ago that he had been sitting at home, waiting for the call that would summon him to go care for employees of the Atomic Energy Commission, or for the UNIDO staff. He reflected on what had happened in the last thirty minutes.

It had been like a scene from a movie. After the wounded terrorist had been transported from the airplane, Carlos had come to thank Rawenduzy for tending to the medical needs of his friend. Then he and the Algerian oil minister left the plane, and Rawenduzy was permitted to take his leave from the hostages still detained in the jet.

Rawenduzy walked down the steps of the gangway, still dressed in his white coat and carrying his medical supply bag in his right hand. Cool air brushed his face, invigorating his senses. Near to the plane stood three men – Carlos, Abdesselam, and a man who Rawenduzy assumed was the Algerian Minister of the Interior. They were engaged in a lively conversation.

Rawenduzy began to walk past them, but Carlos gestured to him that he could not run along just yet.

What now, wondered Rawenduzy? What more did "The Jackal" want from him? Had his delicate mission not yet come to an end? His patient was no longer even in sight. This was strange.

"I demand a private jet so that the physician can return to Vienna at once," Carlos's words were strident, and he sounded impatient.

Rawenduzy could not believe his ears. No. Anything but this. Naturally, he wanted to go home as quickly as possible, but he most certainly did not wish to do so in an aircraft chartered by the terrorists.

"Thank you very much," Rawenduzy cut in. "That is very considerate of you. But I'm perfectly comfortable returning to Vienna on a regular flight."

Rawenduzy did not wait for the Algerian Minister of the Interior to react. Under no circumstances did he wish to travel in a private plane. He politely said goodbye to the trio and hurried into the airport building.

Allah be praised. That had gone well.

The door to the VIP room was open, and Rawenduzy entered. Inside there was a huge glass window that allowed a view of the crowd in the passenger hall. The doctor hardly looked at the people. Exhausted, he dropped into one of the comfortable chairs and took a deep breath.

"Would you like something, Monsieur?" A friendly waiter leaned forward, smiling courteously.

Would he like something? He would like many things, Rawenduzy mused silently, chuckling to himself. Did this person, properly dressed in black, have the slightest notion that he, a doctor of internal medicine from Austria, was at this moment somehow celebrating his second birth? No. And why should he?

"Un verre de jus d'orange, si'il vous plait," responded Rawenduzy. A glass of orange juice, please.

Rawenduzy had not even finished his orange juice when a man approached him and greeted him respectfully and in Arabic. The man had a strong French accent and was difficult to understand. After a few minutes, Rawenduzy understood that this was the Chief of the Airport Police.

He extended Rawenduzy an invitation to lunch. Rawenduzy accepted gladly. His stomach was completely empty. He could not even remember when he had last eaten. His body's clock seemed entirely out of order, and the enormous strain he had been under had apparently blocked out any craving for food.

In a flash, he took off his white coat. From here on out he was just a normal person. At least, so he thought until the food arrived.

The waiting staff appeared with a variety of Arabian delicacies, both cold and warm, and fresh dates for dessert. Rawenduzy decided he might have to reconcile himself to the fate of not being quite a normal person again just yet.

When would the next airplane leave for Vienna, he asked the Chief of the Airport Police.

"Later," said the Algerian, smiling with a non-committal air. Rawenduzy supposed that would have to suffice for now.

Then lunch break was over, and the meal had been cleared. The Chief of Police excused himself and hurried away. Rawenduzy, his senses revived and in good spirits after the abundant meal, got up and went into the passenger hall.

There must be an arrivals and departures board, he thought. Especially departures. He did not want to waste any more time. He was longing for a shower and his cozy bed. To sleep. Simply to sleep his fill would be wonderful.

Damn. Wherever he looked, he saw no sign of information about arriving or departing airplanes. Was he just fatigued? Was his perception playing tricks on him?

Rawenduzy scanned the crowd and saw a small group of pilots. They were all dressed in dashing, dark uniforms. The sleeves of their tailor-made jackets bore golden stripes, and their insignia was clearly displayed on their shoulders. They wore caps, smartly placed on their heads, and the whole costume gave the men a daredevilish appearance.

They seemed to be in excellent moods, and were conversing in German.

"Excuse me," asked Rawenduzy, approaching the pilots. "Could you please tell me when the next aircraft will leave for Vienna?"

The pilots turned around, puzzled.

"Dr. Rawenduzy!" one of them cried. "What are you doing here? What are you doing on the ground? We thought you were in the air, or with the hostages in the airplane."

They came forward cheerfully and shook hands with Rawenduzy. Rawenduzy realized that he was neither wearing his white coat nor carrying his medical supply bag, and yet the men had recognized him.

Rawenduzy was somewhat touched, but now he could not grasp the public impact of his recent actions. He could not assess what it meant within the news media or the world at large. He was still far too wrapped up in it all emotionally, and space and time still felt far too closely interwoven with the distance between here and his normal world.

At any rate, the pilots were thrilled that they had accidentally gotten to meet Rawenduzy, and one of them explained that they had come to Algiers on a private jet of the German magazine Stern. The plane's next destination was Vienna, and they would be delighted if the Kurdish doctor would accompany them.

"That would be wonderful," Rawenduzy said. "Thank you so much for your offer." He no longer had any worries. He needed only to fetch his belongings from the VIP lounge, and this would take only a few moments.

"How dare you!" The passenger hall was filled with a booming voice. "You are forbidden to give an interview here!" The Chief of Airport Police was running towards Rawenduzy, enraged, inflated, and gesticulating wildly with his muscular hands. The German pilots stepped back, appalled. The man was raving in Arabic, so they understood nothing, but his body language spoke for itself.

Rawenduzy could hardly suppress his annoyance, no matter how tired and uninterested in conflict he was, and a loud and violent dispute immediately erupted between him and the Chief of Police. Rawenduzy tried to explain to the Chief of the Police that he had given no interview. He had merely inquired as to when the next plane would leave for Vienna. Rawenduzy also pointed out to the angry Algerian that he had earlier asked the Chief of Police for the same information and had still not received it. Rawenduzy returned to the VIP lounge, upset by the man's ignorance. Inside the lounge, waiting for him, was Dr. Manfred Scheich, the Austrian Ambassador to Algeria.

The entire matter had been very uncomfortable for Rawenduzy. How could this man dare to treat him like this? Why was all this fuss necessary? Try as he might he could see absolutely no reason for it.

They arrived in the VIP lounge, and Rawenduzy took a deep breath as the Ambassador stepped forward to greet him.

"Scheich is the name," said the man, smiling. "Yes, you have heard correctly. Scheich, as in 'sheik' in Arabic."

Scheich wore a tailored, khaki-colored suit. He had a distinguished appearance and an elegant way of speaking, and he radiated the experience of a prudent diplomat. Rawenduzy, still excited by the pompous behavior of the Chief of Police, tried to explain to Scheich that he was not a prisoner and should not be treated like one, and that anyway he had not given an interview. The Kurd insisted that Scheich convey this in French.

"Apparently, this man has no command of high Arabic!" concluded Rawenduzy. And that was that.

The Chief of Police arrived in the VIP lounge, and Scheich exchanged some calm words with him in French, whereupon the Algerian left without a word.

From this moment on, Scheich did not leave the physician's side. He had a telex sent to Mrs. Edith Rawenduzy in Vienna announcing her husband's return and assuring her that he was well. He gave Rawenduzy a ticket for a regular Swissair flight via Zurich to Vienna. The doctor would be spared additional time waiting in Algiers.

The Austrian Ambassador accompanied the Kurdish physician into the plane and promised to inform Vienna of his arrival time. Then Scheich took his leave, stopping to thank Rawenduzy for the doctor's heroic mission.

Relieved, Rawenduzy reclined in his comfortable seat.

"Please fasten your seatbelts and extinguish cigarettes." The pleasant voice of the flight attendant filled the cabin. She had an unmistakable Swiss accent.

The plane accelerated, and soon the giant metal bird was racing faster and faster down the runway. It was marked with the Swiss coat of arms, a white cross on a red background. Then the vibrating aircraft left the ground and began to ascend. The roar of the engines was music to Rawenduzy's ears. It was the music of life, the music of freedom. A music that united the world and touched heaven's infinity.

Rawenduzy did not look out the window. In his heart, he was already in Vienna. How would he get home from the airport? His car was still at the hospital. A taxi. Yes, he could get to the hospital by taxi and from there drive home in his car. Allah be praised, he had no baggage. Only his medical supply bag. In addition, at the hospital he could return the white coat they had lent him.

"Would you like coffee or tea, sir?" A flight attendant leaned towards him, flashing an engaging smile with flawless white teeth. Her blue eyes radiated, tearing the tired doctor from his daydreaming. Disoriented, he quickly chose tea.

Soon meals were served, and the flight attendant brought Rawenduzy cold chicken and salad, with a small piece of cake for dessert.

Throughout the journey the flight attendant returned repeatedly, ready to satisfy even the slightest wish Rawenduzy might have. Orange juice, apple juice, whisky or champagne... whatever the doctor wanted. This passenger was a VIP. He was under the protection of the Austrian government, and was to be made absolutely comfortable. This had been the crew's explicit order.

It was late in the afternoon when the Swissair jet landed at Zurich's Kloten Airport.

One, two three. With a quick step time is running, and we are running with it

Rawenduzy smiled as he remembered the rhyme by Wilhelm Busch. Many times had he read Busch's stories to his son. The story was about two bad boys and all their pranks. Rawenduzy's son would listen to the story attentively, and then would playful recite the lines later, always laughing happily as he did so.

This was the first prank. However, the second prank will follow at once.

And so on, until the poem ended with:

Now the pranks are done.

"I hope you've had an enjoyable flight, and we look forward to welcoming you on board again soon." The now familiar female voice came through the intercom for the last time.

The passengers left their seats and headed for the exit. As Rawenduzy descended the gangway, he savored the memory of a final charming smile from the flight attendant. He proceeded with the other passengers to passport control and customs.

Passport control. His passport. Suddenly he was nervous again. In fact, he thought he must be at his wit's end.

What was he to do? He did not have his passport with him. Do not panic, he thought. What could possibly happen? In the worst case, the authorities would have to contract the Austrian General Consul in Zurich.

His physician's license, he thought. With this document, at least he could prove his identity. Would this be enough? No, of course not. Rawenduzy thought himself an incorrigible optimist and laughed at his thoughts. The whole concept of passports would turn into a farce if a person could just cross political borders with a professional license.

"Your passport, please," said the Swiss border agent. Rawenduzy handed him his physician's ID. The man did not blink an eye. Rawenduzy made an imploring gesture towards his medical supply bag and the white coat hanging from his arm.

"You see," he stammered. "I have just come directly from Algiers. I forgot to take my passport. There were compelling circumstances, you see."

Dr. Rawenduzy was annoyed with himself. Why had he not remembered his passport? But then again, he had not even been home before leaving. Actually, what was he worrying about? In truth, he did not feel the slightest bit guilty.

He was just tired. Extremely, extremely tired. He realized suddenly that he had gone roughly forty hours without sleep. And now he had what seemed to be an intractable problem with a stubborn representative of the Swiss government.

"I'm afraid I cannot let you pass," said the border agent. The man had a typical Swiss accent.

The border agent paused, almost as if for effect. "Unless..." he said.

Slowly, centimeter by centimeter, he slid Rawenduzy's physician's ID back across the narrow counter.

"'Unless?" Rawenduzy repeated, forgetting to breathe.

"Unless," the Swiss agent continued, as if about to clarify a special rule in the border code. The man paused again, and then his stern glance changed to one of anticipation, and then without warning into a friendly grin.

"Unless you immediately tell me the whole story," said the Swiss agent. "I am dying to hear about these terrorists and that flight to Algiers."

Rawenduzy inhaled sharply. He didn't know whether to laugh or cry; he was edgy and really in no mood for jokes.

"You want me to talk about this now?" he half exploded. "In a few sentences? It's impossible!" He shook his head sharply. What nerve this man had, he thought.

"Then you have a nice trip home, and give Vienna a hug for me," said the Swiss, still smiling. The border agent put his right hand to his forehead and saluted Rawenduzy, and with another friendly smile, he motioned Rawenduzy through the gate. Relieved, the Kurd put away his medical license and followed the other passengers into the departure lounge.

He was in Zurich-Kloten, he repeated to himself. He was in Zurich. In Switzerland. Yes, he was in Switzerland. It was over. All over. He was free. Free.

A bit of an Arabic poem came to mind.

Between Heaven and Hell
The path is thinner than a hair.
There are some that fly to the other side
like a strong-winged falcon.
There are some that anxiously weep in fear
of the menacing fire.
And there are those who plunge into hell,
and never reach Paradise …

"Dr. Rawenduzy, please come to the information desk. Dr. Rawenduzy to the information desk, please." The shrill announcement cut through the hall. Rawenduzy did not even notice it till the second time it was made. He was far too immersed in his thoughts. Strong emotions had taken hold of him.

What was the matter now, he wondered?

He was confused. Perhaps they had changed their minds and decided a medical license was not enough to enter Switzerland after all.

Allah have mercy on me, he thought. The road back to Vienna is very rocky.

He made his way through the crowd of people.

The kind woman at the information desk looked up when the Kurdish doctor gave his name. She smiled broadly and informed him that a certain Mr. Peter Nidetzky from the Austrian Radio and Television Corporation was waiting for him.

"Where?" he asked, perplexed.

She pointed across the hall, to a young, medium-sized man. Rawenduzy approached the young man, exchanging glances with the bewildered doctor.

Nidetzky began to speak at once. He was bubbling with questions, and it was difficult for Rawenduzy to follow the journalist's words. To make matters worse, the hall was very noisy, and Rawenduzy was exhausted.

"I have come to meet you in Zurich," Nidetzky said. "The ORF (Austrian Radio and Television Corporation) is planning a live interview upon your arrival in Vienna. It will be held right at the airport. It is better to discuss the details on the flight back. This will give us enough time for you to go over the questions beforehand. It's best you review the questions first because the interview will be conducted live."

The ORF reporter took out his notes and mentioned casually that at least one hundred journalists, from Austria and from around the world, would be waiting for Rawenduzy when the Kurdish physician arrived at Schwechat airport in Vienna. Rawenduzy was overwhelmed by this news. For some reason people seemed to think he was important, both as a physician and a human being.

The Kurd nodded his acquiescence. Nidetzky gently guided him into the VIP lounge. They had espressos, double, of course, and cool, sparkling mineral water.

Rawenduzy felt relieved, and he and Nidetzky struck up a stimulating dialogue. Time flew, and soon the flight to Vienna was announced. They passed through the border control without problems, and without showing passports. It seemed all doors were open to the press, especially to the ORF and their guest.

On the plane, a light snack was offered. Rawenduzy was not hungry. He stuck with coffee and mineral water for the stimulation they offered. Soon even the slightest trace of exhaustion had left him. Fully focused, he answered all of the reporter's questions, leaving out no essential details.

What exactly had happened in the airplane, asked the reporter. How did he succeed in getting the injured terrorist to Algiers alive? What kind of rapport had he had with the individual terrorists? In which language had he communicated with them? Did he have any comments about the female terrorist? What had happened in Algiers?

At the end came the unavoidable, final question. Had the Austrian Chancellor made the right decision?

Repeatedly Nidetzky emphasized that the press had been reporting nonstop on the terrorist attack since its beginning. Real news, however, had been sparse. For example, now all that was really known of events since Rawenduzy departed the plane was that the terrorists and their hostages had continued their flight to Tripoli.

Rawenduzy could not adequately answer the questions as to the abductors' names, but he passed on his suppositions. The Palestinian who had guarded him, and the wounded man had been called Jussuf. Then there was Carlos, also known as Salem, a second man known as Khalid, and probably a Lebanese man called Josef. The woman he believed to have been named "Naaima". Last but not least, there was the wounded terrorist, Henry.

Nidetzky said that all bulletins and reports about the OPEC attack had also included the story of Dr. Wiriya Rawenduzy, the specialist for internal medicine. In the eyes of the media and the world, his courage and fearlessness in voluntarily treating the injured terrorist on the plane were exemplary, and had been essential to the solution to this drama. Furthermore, the doctor had done all this in an airplane in the hands of heavily armed terrorists, packed with explosives, and flying to an unknown destination, an airplane in which high-ranking hostages were being held, almost scared out of their wits for fear of losing their lives.

Rawenduzy was absorbed in his conversation with Nidetzky, and he hardly noticed that the plane was landing in Vienna's Schwechat airport. Suddenly he became silent and turned to the window. The airplane rolled slowly toward the airport complex. The wet, gray landing strip was covered with snow. Inside the airport, a small crowd was waiting.

Waiting for a single man.

Please Take a Bow

"A few minutes ago, Dr. Wiriya Rawenduzy landed in Vienna at Schwechat International Airport. He traveled here from Algiers via Zurich. Peter Nidetzky accompanied him on the last stretch of his flight. We will interview Dr. Rawenduzy, the physician who cared for the injured terrorist on the hijacked flight from Vienna to Algiers, at the beginning of The Daily News tonight. I will try to reach Peter Nidetzky now."

The ORF reporter, properly dressed as always, his face reflecting the stress of the events surrounding the terror attack at the OPEC building, had been given forty minutes to focus on this special report. Thousands of people, both from within Austria and from foreign countries, would be following this program. People across the world were holding their breath, trying to analyze the horror that had unfolded. In the meantime, the crisis was still unfolding; all of the oil ministers plus the Austrian Airlines pilots were still being detained by the killers, and according to the latest press releases, the terrorists had directed the pilots of the ill-fated aircraft to land in Tripoli, the capital of Libya.

However, Rawenduzy, now back in Vienna, felt as if he had been given his life for a second time, and he had consciously accepted it. Humbly. Gratefully. He knew he was no hero. Just a man of action.

And did he enjoy risk? No. Indeed not. Never had he harbored such illusions.

Rawenduzy and Nidetzky headed for the VIP lounge, a cluster of journalists practically glued to them. Time was at a premium: a live interview was scheduled for the second edition of the Daily News. They reviewed the questions as they hurried through the airport.

Press Conference at Vienna Schwechat Airport. December 22, 1975

Cameras clicked. Microphones appeared, seemingly everywhere. Bright lights glared, almost painful to the eyes. The floor was covered with black cables and somehow resembled a snake pit.

Rawenduzy felt his energy wane. Then he saw the crowds mobbing the VIP lounge, and his face turned pale. What could all these people want from him? He had only done his duty. Allah have mercy on me, he thought.

Exhausted, he dropped into a chair. Someone offered him a glass of cold water, and he eagerly drank it.

"Dr. Rawenduzy, are you OK?" Nidetzky looked worried.

"Yes, of course," Rawenduzy said. "When will we begin?"

"In two minutes. Are you ready?"

Rawenduzy composed himself. He nodded and quickly stood up, still rapt in thought. He touched his hair. Every spotlight in the room was directed towards him, the camera crews scrambling to avoid a disruptive glare from his dark, horn-rimmed spectacles. Rawenduzy did not even notice that the temperature in the room had risen. He concentrated fully on the matter at hand.

Suddenly the crowd fell silent, and a red light flickered onto the camera. The live interview was about to begin.

"Paging Peter Nidetzky," a small loudspeaker called across the terminal. Everything was ready. There was no turning back now.

"This is Peter Nidetzky from the VIP lounge inside the Vienna International Airport. It is now 9:42 PM. Sixteen minutes ago, Austrian Airlines flight OS222 from Zurich landed here on time. On that plane was Dr. Rawenduzy, who has returned from an adventure."

In short, concise sentences, the ORF reporter summarized the events of the terrorist attack, skillfully presenting Rawenduzy as the most essential and decisive factor of all the factors that helped to solve the problems while the terrorists were still in Vienna. Then Nidetzky posed his first question.

"What made you come to the heroic decision to participate in the flight this morning?"

The Kurdish doctor explained his feelings in a few sentences, seeming calm and stressing emphatically that the hostages' lives had been at stake. A quick decision had had to be made, without egocentricity or sentimentality.

The interview was breathtaking, and it proceeded on an unavoidable course. Rawenduzy was able to answer efficiently every question the journalists asked. However, it was difficult, and Rawenduzy was grateful that Nidetzky had briefed him prior to the program. Sometimes when he was under mental strain he began to think in Kurdish or Arabic, which could lead him to forget some of the rules of German grammar. Privately, he even admitted to himself that he had still not mastered the three different articles in German – der, die, and das. It amused him to no end.

At home, television viewers hung on the two speakers' every word, torn between two sets of feelings. On one hand, people were disturbed and angry about the horrors of the last few days. The attack on the OPEC Headquarters had caused extreme concern. People had been discussing it day and night, in stores and in offices, all over town. The normal pre-Christmas festivity had turned into confusion, hypotheses, opinions, speculations. Everybody had something to say about everything.

On the other hand, people had become curious. They wanted to know more about this man, this Viennese doctor who was not actually Viennese. What did he look like? Why had he volunteered? What were his motives? It was said that he was married and the father of two small children. Did his actions not show irresponsibility towards his family? In addition, he spoke several languages, including Arabic – had this been of any advantage to him throughout the crisis?

Almost automatically, the Austrian population had begun to take pride in this man, and in the manner in which he had demonstrated nerves of steel throughout this national crisis. He was a man, like you or I, people said. He was a man who could be our neighbor. It was easy for people to identify with Rawenduzy. He displayed no superstar behavior. He was not a smart-aleck, or some arrogant favorite of the moment. No, he was simply a man, worthy of respect. During the interview, he even admitted his weakness and fear.

The ORF program concluded with the thunderous applause of the people assembled in the VIP lounge. Nidetzky thanked Rawenduzy for his willingness to answer so many questions, even after all of the hardship he had endured.

It was only some days later that the physician learned that close to five hundred million people from around the world had watched his interview. After the interview, journalists from Austria and from foreign countries had begun to pose additional questions, many regarding specific problems. Rawenduzy kept his strength and answered all of the questions precisely. This lasted for about an hour, but by then the fatigue had begun to take hold of him, and the stress of the interview worsened the fatigue. Soon his brow was covered with sweat, and his light sweater clung to his trunk. He did not even notice it.

Slowly, the tension eased. Two police officers offered to take him home from the airport. Rawenduzy remembered his car. He had left it at the hospital. In addition, he wanted to give Dr. Steinbereithner a detailed medical report on the successful mission. In addition, he still had to return the white doctor's coat he had borrowed.

Therefore, to the car they went. They raced through town, and in about a half an hour they reached the AKH (Public General Hospital). Rawenduzy's car was still parked where he had left it. No one had towed it away. The police officers stayed in their cars, intending to wait and escort Rawenduzy to Donaustadt, where he lived, but the physician thanked them and declined the police escort. He wanted, finally, to be alone. He had had enough. He had begun to hate all of the attention that had been placed on him.

He entered the hospital quickly. Steinbereithner was waiting for him, and the head of the Intensive Care Unit congratulated the Kurd on his courage as a human being and on his efficiency as a physician. The Austrian doctor nearly even managed to sound friendly. Steinbereithner and Rawenduzy exchanged medical information for a few minutes, and then Rawenduzy excused himself. He was just too tired and worn out to do anything else. He handed over the doctor's coat, politely said goodbye, and hurried to his car.

Inside his car, a feeling of home washed over him. Each part of the car symbolized security, from the stick shift, to the steering wheel, to the seat coverings. The smell of the car was so familiar. Slowly and consciously, he turned the ignition key. The engine gave off a satisfied sound. He turned on the lights and eased the car into first gear. The car obeyed instantly, and soon the heavy automobile was moving leisurely and even somewhat sleepily down the road.

Rawenduzy enjoyed it immensely. As he drove, he loved the traffic lights, even the red ones that prolonged his journey home. On the radio, soft music was playing. The night was dark, and not a single star could be seen. It did not bother him. An indescribable feeling of happiness had taken possession of his soul. It was overwhelming.

His thoughts drifted to his father. Today his father would have been proud of his first-born son. And there in the car an imaginary cloak at night somehow wrapped itself around him.

And he knew that he, like every other Kurd, was a son of Saladin.

And he knew that, in all he had been through, life had protected him.

The Past in the Present

The well-known Viennese psychiatrist Erwin Ringel once said: "Is it not disastrous if we let our lives just pass us by, depriving ourselves of life, and existing as prisoners of our own unawareness?"

As a physician and as a human being, Ringel stood up strongly for peace in modern education. It seemed especially important to him that psychotherapy be socially responsible. For him, catch phrases such as "intervention" and "involvement" were not mere lip service. During his life, he gave numerous lectures and published often, despite being severely handicapped, and he never tired of exhorting people to open both their eyes and their hearts at the same time. He believed that:

If we overcome passivity, we can achieve the following: We can expand our milieu. We can improve our existing relationships, as well as activate new ones. We can discover new values, increase our openness, and remove narrow-mindedness. We can create an atmosphere of trust.

I was privileged to know Ringel personally. I was associated with him only briefly, during my tenure as Secretary General at the Austrian Red Cross Youth. He was, and still is, even now posthumously, a symbol of encouragement for me personally, and a living image of what it means to affirm life.

Because of his example, I tried to examine the motives of Dr. Wiriya Rawenduzy during his involvement in the OPEC crisis with a critical eye. What reasons did Rawenduzy have for doing what he did? What criteria led to such a decision? Was there another impetus, something not yet defined or articulated that triggered this action of self-sacrifice?

Could no other doctor really have been found? Was the decision to risk his own life based upon an undigested syndrome often found in foreigners? Was this daring undertaking meant to justify his being an Austrian, or even to express gratitude to Austria for taking him in? Was a person born Kurdish in Iraq considered a second-class person? And could racism have led Rawenduzy to decide to risk his life for his new country, the racism present on subtle levels both then and now, yet denied publicly and politically,?

How should we judge Rawenduzy's attitude towards his family? Do the needs of the country overshadow personal moral obligations? Do they eliminate them? What would the consequences have been had he died on that day in 1975?

Last but not least, was Rawenduzy offered any kind of a monetary reward for his actions? Had the politicians sought to pay Rawenduzy off in order to wash their hands of responsibility for the event? Had they complied with the terrorists' demands simply because they wished to dispose of this delicate problem by removing the terrorists from Austrian soil as soon as possible?

Rawenduzy was more than willing to answer my penetrating questions. Repeatedly I tried to discover the man he was inside. I had to be tactful; I did not want to wound the dignity of this courageous man. Nevertheless, the complete truth of this matter was vital to me.

The physician never tired. He sought to explain every detail, repeatedly pointing out the steps taken and why they were necessary in the context of the situation.

It seemed to me that when he made his decisions Rawenduzy forgot completely about spectacular daring or low-order sensationalism.

Rawenduzy calmly explained that his attitude toward Austria should not be thought of as meek. That was not why he had done what he had done. He had simply been concerned for the hostages, and there hadn't seemed to be any other alternatives. After all, the terrorists had threatened to blow up the OPEC Headquarters several times. There had to be an immediate stop to this human tragedy; there could not be another bloodbath. The lives of the hostages had been exposed to extreme danger, and this situation unconditionally demanded whatever protection was possible.

In addition, Rawenduzy had made a promise to Bruno Kreisky, and this reinforced his decision to take part in the mission.

Rawenduzy repeatedly emphasized that he had never been the victim of any racism in Austria, except for when he had been a student searching for a room.

Rawenduzy also reminded me that he spoke Arabic. He was familiar with the Arab mind. It seemed to him quite logical and obvious that he should volunteer to interpret and to help medically.

He would do it again. Most certainly.

Moreover, when he made his decision Rawenduzy had understood completely the terrorists' demands regarding their wounded comrade. This was clearly a political, not a medical problem. Yet it was a shame and a scandal that neither representatives of the government nor members of the diplomatic corps were able to find a surgeon willing to volunteer in this dramatic situation. The authorities attempted to justify it by the date. It was, after all, only two days before Christmas, and the 'gods in white' were no longer in Vienna. They had already left for their well-deserved vacations, with or without their families.

Speaking of family, Rawenduzy had never seen a connection between the decision to fly with the terrorists and his responsibility toward his family. Even before the difficult operation began, he had never doubted in the least that he would return home in the evening. A positive attitude was and still is a basic part of Wiriya Rawenduzy's personality, and countless examples attest to it.

"I am sorry. I cannot answer this question!" Rawenduzy bursts out laughing, looking at me almost compassionately.

Dr. Rawenduzy with his wife and Interior Minister Rösch.

With Bruno Kreisky (left) and Rihad Al-Azawi, “The Negotiator”.

With Ambassador Nettel and Minister Staribacher

Bruno Kreisky thanks Dr. Rawenduzy and presents him with the Republic of Austria's Silver Star of High Honor.

"I was never in a situation where I was given money, or where I had to refuse it. It was never offered to me. Not even a single Groschen (a unit of Austrian currency at the time, the equivalent of a fraction of a cent)."

In spite of the multitude of reporters present, no one made even the slightest attempt to thank this brave physician with a monetary reward.

"Were you disappointed?" I ask.

"No," he says. "Quiet honestly, no. I probably would not have accepted it, although in those days I practically had to turn each Schilling (Austrian currency at the time) twice to make ends meet. Remember in those days I was on duty at the Vienna Health Insurance Services, as well as at the Austrian Red Cross. In addition, I had a modest office in Kaisermühlen (part of a Viennese district). As the sole breadwinner in the family it was often very difficult for me to take care of my financial responsibilities."

"Regardless of this," Rawenduzy continues. "My motive for what I did was simply helping and serving my fellow men. This is what I think. This is what I live. This is what I am."

Rawenduzy takes off his glasses and puts them down. I do not avoid his glance. Silence fills the comfortable living room of his house. For some time now, we have met here, rather than in a coffee house in the city. In the coffee houses, there had been just too much babble of voices, which made it difficult to take notes. There had been too much noise, which made it difficult for Rawenduzy to remember anything. There had been too many distractions, which made it difficult to get access to Rawenduzy's feelings about the deepest human issues.

I look at Rawenduzy, and it seems he expects me to give my opinion about his motivations for doing what he did. However, I am having trouble finding words. Normally I have no problem finding and using poignant arguments. I have studied philosophy, and am accustomed to framing my thoughts into words. Yet now I remain steadfastly silent. What would I say? Any comment I could make would be superfluous and would sound banal.

"What is life?" Rawenduzy says. His voice sounds suddenly familiar, and it pulls me out of my momentary passivity. Rawenduzy is moved, and he is reciting Erich Fried:

Anger at injustice is not enough.
We have to examine it thoroughly,
and do something about it.
That is life.

I nod in agreement. Injustice. OK, I think, so examine it.

I try to summarize. "Much time has gone by since the terror attack. Illich Ramirez Sanchez, alias Carlos, was arrested many years later, and is now serving a life sentence in a French prison. The terrorist by the name of Hans-Joachim Klein, the man whose life you saved, lived underground in France for more than twenty years. The international authorities eventually caught him a little more than four years ago. He was extradited to Germany, where a court found him guilty. He is now serving out his sentence in a maximum security prison."

"The female actor of this horror story," I continue, "was actually a woman named Gabriele Kröcher-Tiedemann, a German. She was set free due to insufficient evidence, and died in 1995."

"Do you know of any additional issues," I ask, "regarding the Arabs, specifically?"

"Most certainly," Rawenduzy replies. He rises from his comfortable armchair and disappears for a few minutes. I wonder what other information he could possibly provide. Deep in thought, I reach for my cup of tea. With milk. At heart I am an Anglophile, but espresso Macchiato is still my favorite beverage.

While I am sipping my tea and wondering if I should flavor it with a second spoonful of sugar, the master of the house returns to the room. He carries in his hand a black folder. I cannot help but notice that he is smiling, somewhat triumphantly.

"Look what I found," he says. "This is an issue of an Arabic weekly newspaper called Al-Waset, published in London. In the November 2000 issue, they published the life story of a Palestinian by the name of Anis Al-Nakasch, who was in fact the true head of the terrorist group that attacked the OPEC building in Vienna. His name within his organization was Khalid."

"What do you mean he was the head of the gang?" I protest. "But that was Carlos. He was the boss. He conducted the negotiations. He was the one laying out the conditions and demands." I am being rather outspoken, interrupting Rawenduzy's explanations. "What does this mean?" I demand. "We have read and heard so much about Carlos, yet suddenly we discover he was only second fiddle? I cannot believe this."

My personal physician takes a deep breath and asks me to hear him out. I am painfully aware that I am being indirectly scolded, and I fall silent. Inwardly, I am rebelling. Why am I writing this story if Carlos may have been insignificant?

In the November 20, 2000 edition of Al-Waset, Al-Nakasch describes his career. He began his political-terrorist activities in the Fatah organization. He was a "warrior for the freedom of the Palestinians", not only the leader of the group but also the man in charge of the OPEC attack. In detail, he presents the reasons for, as well as the preparation, execution, and consequences of the terrorist attack in Vienna in 1975.

The radical Palestinian group centered around Wadi e Haddad conceived the plan for the operation while they were in Aden, Yemen. The reason was simple. The group needed money. A lot of money. They believed that if they abducted the oil ministers of Saudi Arabia and Iran they would be able to make off with ten million dollars in ransom money. The plan was that even though the ransom money was paid, both of the ministers were to be killed in Vienna.

Al-Nakasch had been in Vienna several times. He had even been into the OPEC Headquarters in order to prepare for the attack. He was exclusively responsible for the operation, and consequently the negotiations, but it was nevertheless decided at a meeting with Carlos in Beirut that Carlos would become involved and would issue the orders to the authorities. At that meeting, it was further decided that two Germans, a man and a woman, as well as a Palestinian called Jussuf and a Lebanese man by the name of Josef, were to participate.

Al-Nakasch goes on to describe the procedure of the attack. In the last phase prior to the attack, the evening before the operation, the group met between 6:00 PM and 7:00 PM in a square close to the Vienna State Opera. Two days before December 21, two members of the Red Brigade delivered the weapons. The final briefings took place the night prior to the attack at a hotel in Vienna.

The following day the terrorists took a streetcar to the OPEC building. Two of them carried athletic bags. They knew that police officers guarded the entrance gate to the building. In a friendly tone, they asked the guards where the oil ministers were holding their meeting. The police officers supplied the information willingly, obviously thinking the unobtrusive killers were journalists. Al-Nakasch sounds almost cynical as he describes how the terror group was escorted to the first floor by police officers. When the terrorists arrived in the conference hall, they immediately took it by storm.

The assault was to be carried out by two groups working parallel to each other. Al-Nakasch and two of the other fighters stormed the hall of the oil ministers with their weapons drawn. They shot twice into the air, and everyone dropped to the floor, deadly afraid. Meanwhile, the second group of terrorists took the employees of OPEC into their power.

Despite all of the turmoil, two of the OPEC guards, a Libyan and an Iraqi, thought the woman in the group would be a weakness. They attacked her, but she shot within a fraction of a second and killed them both. A shoot-out with the police ensued, during which the German comrade of the terrorists, the young man called Henry, was severely wounded and rushed to the hospital.

Al-Nakasch describes the treatment of the hostages in detail. The hostages were divided into three groups. The first group consisted of the enemies, the oil ministers from Persia and Saudi-Arabia. The second group was the neutrals, the ministers from Kuwait, Nigeria, Indonesia, Ecuador, Gabon, and Venezuela. The third group was the group of the friends – Algeria, Iraq, and Libya.

According to Al-Nakasch, there were never any serious negotiations between their side and the Austrians. The terrorists requested that Carlos's communiqué be read on the radio, and the request was promptly complied with. Next, they demanded a bus and an airplane, and that the injured terrorist be brought with them. This request considerably delayed matters, but in the end, it was also fulfilled.

The plan further called for each captive oil minister to send a letter to his government or embassy, a letter that was to be delivered without censorship. The terrorists dictated the letters to the representatives of Saudi Arabia and Iran, demanding a ransom payment of $5,000,000 per country. Both of the oil ministers involved knew that they would be shot if their governments did not pay.

However, the terrorists actually wanted to dispose of these two men in Vienna, or at the latest either in Aden or Baghdad, once the money had been transferred.

Al-Nakasch emphasizes that he foresaw difficulties. Because of the peace treaty between Iran and Iraq and the end of the Kurdish uprising, it could pose a problem to execute the Iranian oil minister in Baghdad. In addition, Wadi e Haddad had his base in Aden; therefore, Aden would not be an appropriate place for an execution.

Al-Nakasch emphasizes in his interview that he repeatedly asked for the Ambassador of Libya during the hostage crisis, but to no avail. Next, the Ambassador of Iraq was summoned. Finally, the Chargé d'Affaires of Iraq appeared, and Carlos introduced himself. Up to that point, Carlos had received strict orders to stay in the background. Al-Nakasch was afraid that the authorities would become nervous if they knew that Carlos was involved. Carlos was not only very well known, but was wanted internationally.

On the morning of December 22, the terrorists and their hostages proceeded to the airplane that awaited them. Al-Nakasch remained on the bus with the others, while Carlos went alone into the airplane to inspect it. Carlos confirmed that the authorities had in fact delivered their wounded comrade, and that he was in the care of a Kurdish physician who had volunteered to accompany him on the flight.

Not without satisfaction, Al-Nakasch commented on the end of the drama. The plane flew to Algiers, where the terrorists negotiated with the Algerian government for hours. Then the flight continued to Libya, where it took ages for Mr. Abdul Salam Dschalud, the Prime Minister of Libya, to appear. At this point Carlos expressed to Al-Nakasch that he believed his part of the assignment had been completed, and that Al-Nakasch should now proceed with the operation.

Negotiations with Abdul Salam Dschalud turned out to be difficult. The terrorists requested a Boeing 707 – a long ditance aircraft that they could have flown to Aden – but this request was categorically refused. Al-Nakasch decided to continue on the same plane, and to land in Tunisia first. However, when the terrorists neared Tunisia, the permission to land was denied. They returned to Algiers, and Al-

Nakasch, under pressure from the government, was forced to release the hostages and to surrender. The ransom money, $10,000,000, had already been transferred. The foreign minister of Algeria received the terrorists personally as they left the plane, and the terrorists were taken to a house.

In the end, Al-Nakasch flew to Damascus, and Carlos to Aden. There, Wadi e Haddad put the blame on Carlos for not having followed the orders to shoot the Iranian and Saudi Arabian oil ministers.

Al-Nakasch stresses that Carlos was not a coward. It was just that in the beginning Carlos did not kill for money. That came later in his career.

Rawenduzy slides the newspaper across the small table. I look at the photo, and my face registers disappointment. This cannot be. The head of a terror gang could not possibly look like this. I had formed a picture of my own of the man while Rawenduzy described Al-Nakasch. My picture was of an Al-Nakasch that was grandiose, athletic, and bore strong features. Nothing could have been further from the truth. The real Al-Nakasch had a plump face with a grayish set of spectacles that suggested he was near-sighted. He had a sparse fluff of hair that encircled a broad brow set on a rather bald skull, and his whole appearance reminded me of that of a circus clown. He had a trace of a beard, which was nothing to rave about either.

Carlos looks like a model compared to this person, I think. Of course, comparing the two men is trivial, and completely unnecessary.

"And whatever happened to Khalid?" I ask. I am curious, despite the man's appearance.

"Five years after the OPEC attack, this man was again involved in a terror attack, this time in Paris." Rawenduzy mentions details, and tries to explain to me the political background. "Schapur Bachtiar was the last Prime Minister of Shah Reza Pahlewi of Iran. When the Shah was overthrown by Ayatollah Ruhollah Khomeini in 1979, the result was that the new regime wanted to kill Schahpur Bachtiar. Bachtiar fled to Paris, where an assassination attempt on him failed in 1980. In connection with this crime, Al-Nakasch was arrested and sentenced to life in prison for having murdered a police officer. However, ten years after he was convicted, the new Iranian regime entered into negotiations with the government of France and succeeded in obtaining the release of the prisoner."

The fire in Rawenduzy's eyes seems to have gone out for a moment, and his countenance shows growing discomfort. He continues in a hoarse voice.

"And now the inconceivable part of this whole story. In all the years that Nakasch spent in prison in France, his true identity, and thus his life story, never became known. None of the many secret services involved in the case succeeded in learning who the prisoner really was, so they had no idea of the brutal truth of his history and the tremendous danger he posed. And Anis Al-Nakasch remained silent for ten long years."

It is inexcusable, unbelievably abstruse, I think. How should such mistakes be avoided in the future? Should governments legalize more coercive measures, even deadly attacks? Should they round up more people who might be involved in terrorist activities? Or should we call such a case merely a regrettable mistake? If yes, whose mistakes should we blame?

No. Such debate would be nothing more than a paralyzing fantasy. Why argue endlessly? It would be better to share dispassionately the following opinion:

We can almost know everything. Only one thing is impossible: To know what we will know in the future.

From "Klein" to "Alias Henry"

He could have spoken, but he chose not to. He did not want to understand anything, but he understood everything. He wanted help, although an innocent man was risking his life to provide it. He did not wish to show even the slightest gratitude, although he had almost thirty years to do it.

The man in question is Hans-Joachim Klein. Alias "Henry".

He was one of the terrorists who cold-bloodedly attacked the OPEC Headquarters in Vienna shortly before Christmas in 1975. The attack almost ended in a massacre. He was the man who sustained serious injuries in a firefight with the Viennese police.

Hans-Joachim Klein. German.

After he recovered from his wounds in the OPEC attack, Klein went to a training camp in Yemen. After the OPEC operation, a warrant for his arrest was issued, and a reward of several thousand German Marks offered for his capture. As a result, Klein was unable to return to Europe. Wadi e Haddad, the autocratic commander of the terrorist group to which Klein belonged, had decided not to send Klein back to Europe on false papers. He could be captured, and if he testified it would be far too dangerous for the other members of the group.

After spending almost a year training under Wadi e Haddad at the camp, Klein was able to employ skill and cunning to procure a ticket back to Europe. By this time, he had already had enough of terrorism, and was searching for a way out. Unfortunately, he knew too much to be permitted to leave. Above all, he knew too much about the international connections of the group.

It would be far beyond the scope of this book to delve into explicit details of the far-reaching contacts of terrorist groups

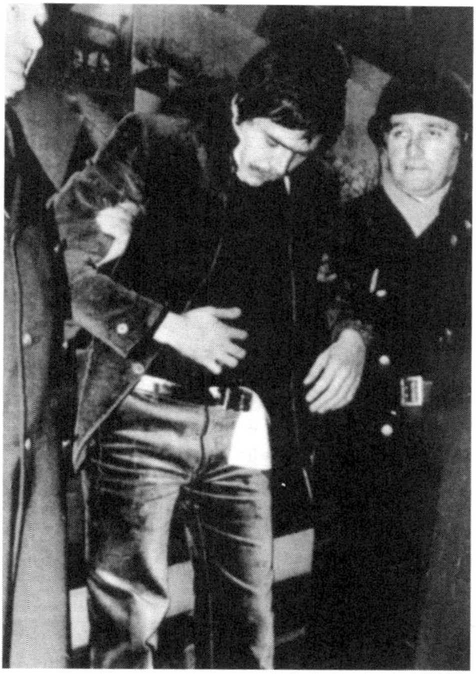

The wounded terrorist, Hans-Joachim Klein

Hans-Joachim Klein is transported to the hospital.

and their intermediaries, and it would lead us far away from our current focus on Hans-Joachim Klein. Therefore, we will stick with Klein's story.

Luckily for him, Klein was successful in leaving the terror organization. He vanished, covered his tracks, and went underground in France, living unnoticed in a village in Normandy for years. He renounced terrorism. In fact, it seemed to be important for him to renounce terrorism publicly. He was able to tell his story in the German magazine "Spiegel", and thus became a true danger to his former colleagues. They tried to eliminate him, but failed.

Klein lived underground for more than twenty years. He existed in a state of constant panic, and authorities report he seemed almost relieved when he was finally caught and arrested in 1998. He was tried for his role in the attack on the OPEC Headquarters in December of 1975, and he was sentenced to fourteen years in prison in Frankfurt am Main, Germany.

When Dr. Rawenduzy began to tell me his of experiences as "The Terrorist's Physician", I was tempted to get in touch with the prisoner Klein, who then sat somewhere in a German prison. I wondered what recollections he would have of Rawenduzy, now after nearly thirty years. Rawenduzy and I often discussed whether it would make sense to contact Klein.

If I did it via an official route, it would mean Sisyphean labor and tremendous strain. I could just see myself addressing countless letters to countless offices in Germany, placing expensive phone call after expensive phone call to foreign countries.

Still, we both believed we should try it. However, how does one start such an effort effectively, when one is based in Vienna? To whom should I address my letter, and where should I send it?

I started by picking up the telephone and dialing the number of the German Embassy in Vienna. The phone was answered by a woman with a friendly voice and a distinct German accent.

I introduced myself and asked timidly if I could speak to someone who could give me information on terrorism in Germany.

"Let me connect you," the woman said. Soon I was speaking to someone else, to whom I repeated my request, and by whom I was again transferred. This procedure was repeated a few times until, within several minutes, I was speaking to the Ambassador himself.

I briefly explained the reason for my call. I reviewed the details of the OPEC assault in Vienna in 1975, adding details on my connection with Dr. Rawenduzy and our interest in the terrorist Klein. I told the Ambassador I wished to conduct an interview for biographical information, and was hoping for a healthy human and journalistic interchange.

"We will be glad to help you," said the Ambassador. "Give me your telephone number. We will call you back. Should you encounter any difficulties, please get in touch with me again. I wish you the best." It was a charming answer.

I could hardly believe it. The whole process had been utterly uncomplicated, and I had not had to provide any personal data. Of course, this could also mean that the Ambassador had not even written down my contact information, and had just been glad to get rid of me. After all, anyone could call with a story like this. Perhaps the Ambassador had thought I was a little crazy.

It was a morning at the end of June. By the end of lunch, I had already forgotten the conversation. Not long after lunch, my cell phone rang.

"Good afternoon," said the voice on the other end. "This is Mr. Arm from the German Embassy. I am the liaison officer for the Federal Bureau of Criminal Investigation, and I have learned of your request regarding the prisoner Klein. I would like to give you the phone number of the Department of

Criminal Law in Wiesbaden. I am sure they can help you locate Klein's prison."

He gave me the phone number immediately, along with the country code for Germany. This was efficiency coupled with unbelievable friendliness. The German official told me to contact him again if there were any problems.

For the second time in a day, I was speechless. What was going on? It must be my lucky day, I thought. Excited, I called Dr. Rawenduzy and informed him that if things continued at such a speed our interview could very well happen soon.

Rawenduzy was skeptical. After all, we were talking about a former terrorist.

The next day I called Wiesbaden, but I had no significant results. I was politely informed that the officials in Wiesbaden were not the correct authorities on such matters, and that I should contact the press office in Karlsruhe. They provided me with a telephone number and an internet address.

From this point on, I was confronted with a labyrinth.

I spoke several times to charming women who asked me to state my request over and over again, promised to call me back, and then never did. Weeks passed by without a word. I continued to call Karlsruhe, but my calls became annoying because they always concluded with meaningless phrases from the secretaries. Finally, I explained to one of them that I could live with it if no information was available, but would appreciate it if they stopped wasting my time with half answers.

The secretary answered that the problem was due to someone being on vacation and a resulting lack of personnel. When she said it, she was quite charming.

I had no comment.

This is exactly like Austria, I fumed. There was no difference. In the past I had often had to work with Austrian authorities and their representatives, both privately and professionally, and it frustrated me just like this did.

Disenchanted, I went on holiday with my family and two foster children from Belarus. I tried to forget about Klein. Did I really need him? What for?

Rawenduzy had sent me off to my well-deserved Italian vacation with his best wishes. He had said he would call me in Italy should there be any news.

The days by the sea flew by. We swam, sunbathed, played games, ate ice cream. We relaxed completely. With my three children around me, I forgot completely about terrorism. In addition, I had been lucky enough to leave my laptop in Vienna.

It was late at night. My husband and I had some refreshments, and soft snoring could be heard from the girls' room.

"What will you do about the Klein case?" my husband, Heinz, asked. "Did you really think they would just hand him to you on a silver platter?"

Heinz was very clear saying that which I had not wanted to face.

"Why don't you just call the German Embassy in Vienna again?" Heinz continued. "The people there promised to help you."

Actually, I thought, he was right. Why hadn't I thought of it before? I decided that my excuse would be that I was acting as a substitute mother and as a result preoccupied with mastering simple Russian expressions. Anyway, where was my calendar? It served as my notebook and it was forever lined with tiny scraps of paper.

I was giddy. I hoped that I had not left it at home. I tore open my handbag and... Yes. There was the dark blue notebook with the golden Arabic trim and the inscription "Arab Bank". This, a gift from my personal physician, was just one of many interesting utensils found in a woman's handbag.

What was the man's name again? Something with an A. It was tiring to search through all of these scraps of paper. Here it was. Criminal Department. Arm. Of course, Mr. Arm. He would help me.

I sat down to enjoy a lemon soda, and soon had made peace with the world. I would call Mr. Arm first thing in the morning. I hoped that he would not be on holiday like I was.

In the morning, we had a large breakfast of cornflakes, with and without milk, panini with prosciutto, soft-boiled eggs, puddings of various flavors, fresh fruit, and orange juice, and soon the girls were racing off to the sea. Their laughter was an amusing mixture of Russian, English, and German, and it echoed in my head as I sat down and dialed the phone number on my cell phone.

"Yes, of course I remember you," said Mr. Arm. "Have you made contact with Klein yet?"

Mr. Arm sounded so close I thought he was standing next to me. His tone was so friendly that I came to the point immediately. I had accomplished nothing. Absolutely nothing.

Mr. Arm immediately promised to take control of the matter, but asked that I should be so kind as to allow him a few days. I was very relieved.

Soon after I returned to Vienna, I received a call from my new benefactor. Arm informed me that Klein was imprisoned in the JVA Schwalmstadt Detention Center, and supplied me with the address and telephone number.

"JVA," I said, interrupting Mr. Arm. "What does that mean?"

"Justizvollzugsanstalt," he said. Institution of Justice. "This sounds better than Knast." Knast is German slang for prison.

I burst out laughing. Of course, JVA did sound better than the word prison.

Mr. Arm had also done research on Klein's lawyers, and had all of their names and telephone numbers. However, for the time being he did not wish to burden me with this. He assured me he would keep them on file in case I needed them in the future.

"All the best, and have fun," he wished me, and said goodbye. His kindness touched me, and I reported my first partial success to Dr. Rawenduzy.

"I will continue to keep my fingers crossed," Dr. Rawenduzy told me. "In the meantime I will think of questions I would like to ask my former involuntary patient. All the best, and goodbye."

Now there was no time to lose. The next day I called Schwalmstadt and talked to the head of JVA Schwalmstadt, Director Hoos.

Hoos was accommodating and friendly, and he asked me to put my request in writing. He would then take all necessary legal steps to make it possible for Rawenduzy and Klein to meet. The single condition was that Klein consent to the interview.

Actually, I had not even thought about this. Why would Klein refuse to talk to us? It would mean meeting the man who saved his life, and personally, I was sure he would want to thank Rawenduzy. I assured Hoos that the subject of terrorism would not be discussed in this meeting; I wanted to focus on the human story.

I quickly wrote a two-page letter to Hoos, and faxed it to him the same day. The internet server at JVA did not work, so it was impossible to send it by email.

The response came the same day. It was devastating, but completely understandable. Mr. Hoos called and informed me that Hans-Joachim Klein had been transferred to JVA Frankfurt and was no longer under his jurisdiction. Hoos asked me not to despair, and promised that he would pass my letter on to his colleague. He assured me that I could count on his support. He reminded me that Klein could very well refuse to talk to us; his verdict had already been commuted to a mitigatory status. In this phase, Klein would be heading for freedom, and would not want any press, no matter how insignificant it appeared.

I trusted Hoos completely. He worked in an easy and open way that fascinated me. Although he did not know me, although we were separated by roughly a thousand kilometers, although we had only spoken on the telephone twice, he had become significantly involved in my effort.

Another week went by, and I received a letter from the head of JVA Frankfurt am Main. I tore open the envelope nervously and let my eyes race over the polite greetings. A few lines down the crucial sentence caught my eye:

"After consulting the above-mentioned prisoner, he is unwilling to be available for an interview while his case is pending."

Commentary and passing remarks about the ex-terrorist Klein's behavior are superfluous. His actions speak for themselves, especially after thirty years. The punch line of the subject of Klein is clear when one reads the title of his book, published in 1979:

"Return to Humanity: The Appeal of a Disillusioned Terrorist"

On the Razor's Edge

It is impossible to suppress the Kurdish revolution forever,
because they are fighting for their lives
and they are willing to pay any price to win.
Pandit Jawaharlal Nehru

For thousands of years, the Kurds have existed within several political regions at once – in the east among the Persians, in the south among the Arabs, and in the north among the Turks and Armenians. These areas originally composed a relatively united Greater Kurdistan, but eventually political revolutions and the founding of new states divided the Kurdish people.

Of the more than thirty million Kurds of various tribes, more than half live in Turkey, about one third in Iran, over four million in Iraq, and the remainder in Syria, Lebanon, and the former Soviet states. In addition, more than a million Kurds live abroad but still identify themselves as members of the Kurdish minority.

Legendary Kurdish leader Mullah Mustafa Barzani (1903-1979)

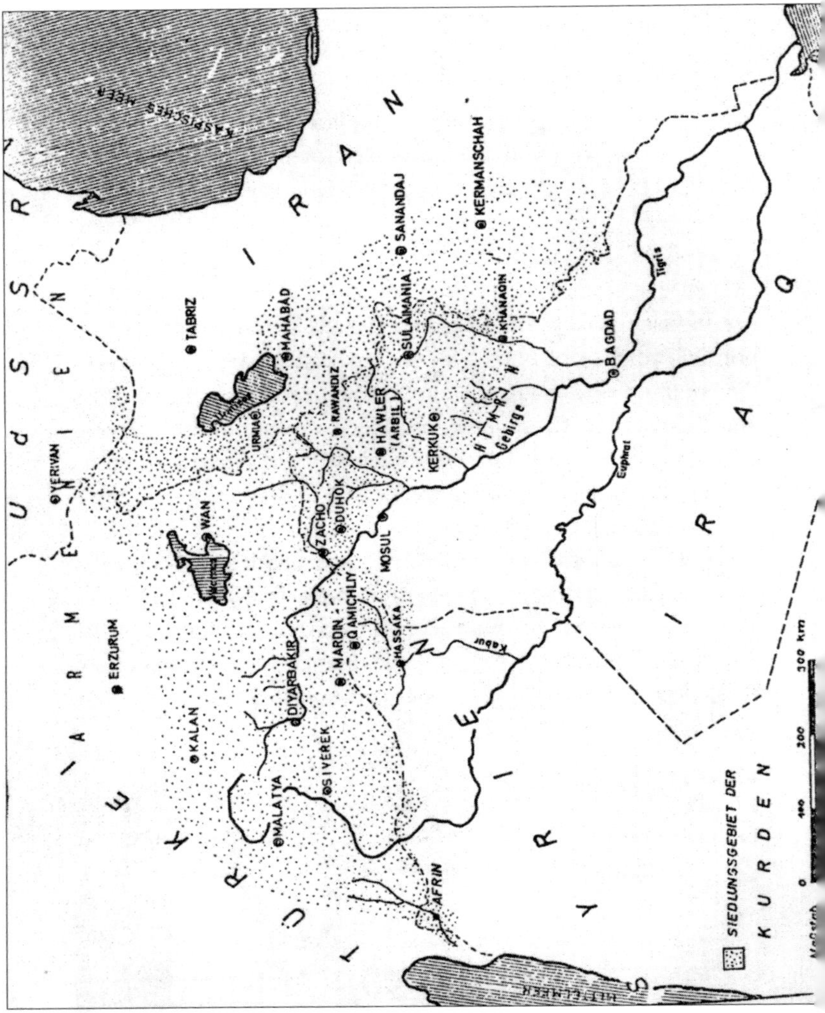

Region of Kurdish settlements in five countries.

Since the abovementioned upheavals, Kurds have been fighting for autonomy in their new states, but they have largely fought in vain. In both Turkey and Iran there has been little or no progress towards independence. In Iraq, the Kurds fought a battle for autonomy and won it in 1970 under General Mustafa Barzani. However, the victory was neither satisfactory nor lasting. Four years later, the Kurds fought a major battle against the Iraqi army. More than sixty thousand Kurds were killed, and the victory of Saddam Hussein's soldiers was decisive and overwhelming.

In 1976, resistance flared up anew. A political party was formed, and the lawyer Mam Jalal Talabani returned from exile in Damascus to become the party's leader. The old Democratic Party of Kurdistan (KDP) was formed anew under the leadership of Massoud Barzani, the son of the legendary general.

Parallel to the events in the Middle East, in Europe Kurdish representatives tried repeatedly to point out the abuses of human rights that were occurring among the Kurds, and to educate the public as to the cruel torture methods employed in Iraq. One of the most important Kurdish representatives in Europe was Dr. Wiriya Rawenduzy.

By 1961, Rawenduzy was already one of the three primary international spokesmen for the Kurdish uprising – in those days the revolt was against the government of General Qassim in Iraq. As mentioned above, Rawenduzy's political activities led the Austrian government to threaten to expel him from Austria, and he was only able to remain in the country because he married an Austrian woman and obtained Austrian citizenship. From then on, his status was clarified, and he gradually withdrew from politics. At least officially.

In reality, he remained involved in the efforts to help his people. He organized several humanitarian shipments, mainly vital medicines for the Kurds, who during the years of the post-1991 embargo were unprotected and at the mercy of Saddam

Hussein. More importantly, Rawenduzy was always the "power behind the throne" of peaceful Kurdish resistance abroad. He was one of the most powerful Kurds in exile in Western Europe, and he worked hard to promote unity and balance among the competing groups in the Kurdish resistance.

This made Rawenduzy a continuing enemy of the Iraqi government, which was a dangerous status to have. In those days, open critics of the Baath regime often lost their lives. Rawenduzy knew this, but fear was foreign to him.

Once Dr. Hennebichler, a historian and friend of Dr. Rawenduzy's, received an invitation to visit Hashim Akrawi, who was then the head of the Kurdish government in Iraq. Akrawi had been put in power by Saddam Hussein in 1976, and was considered a stooge, a Kurd who upheld sham autonomy and pleased those in charge in Baghdad by pulling strings, forging connections, and controlling a puppet parliament.

Hennebichler visited Akrawi, and when he returned to Vienna he sought to share his findings, but discovered that there was an enormous lack of information about the Kurds. Therefore, Hennebichler organized a radio report on the Kurds on ORF (the Austrian Broadcasting Corporation). One of the leading speakers was Dr. Wiriya Rawenduzy. Rawenduzy offered touchy details of the conditions in Iraq, as well as strong statements about Akrawi and his positions. Most notably, Rawenduzy called Akrawi a traitor.

Dire consequences followed. Rawenduzy had known this would happen. After all, he was by blood a Kurd from Iraq, even if he now held an Austrian passport. Now his enemies would be out for blood, because an attempt on his life would finally silence him forever.

It was a typical day in November. Grey clouds hung over Vienna, and at Rawenduzy's office patients silently waited, their moods reflected on their faces. It was close to 4:00 PM when the doorbell rang. The receptionist pressed the button automatically, and the entrance door opened.

Two men in light trench coats entered the hall. The nurse inspected them and, puzzled, asked if hey had an appointment. According to her schedule, she was expecting only an elderly couple. Could she help them?

They replied briefly. They wanted to talk to her boss, and they wanted to talk to him immediately.

The nurse became suspicious, and asked the men to take a seat.

"Thank you, but we would rather stand," they said, and turned their backs on the reception desk.

The nurse quickly picked up the telephone and, speaking in a whisper, informed Rawenduzy of the intruders.

What should she do, she asked him?

Nothing, he replied. He would be out shortly.

"You wish to speak with me," Rawenduzy said a few minutes later. "May I know why?" His voice was harsh and carried a biting undertone; it did not sound at all like Rawenduzy. His hands were buried in the pockets of his white coat, and he wore a stethoscope around his neck. He looked irreproachable. His face radiated displeasure and his eyes were hostile. He hated any kind of disturbance, especially when it came at the expense of his patients.

"Excuse us for disturbing you here," said one of the men, "above all during office hours. My colleague and I are from the State Police. If you wish to see for yourself, please..." The two police officers slowly took out their ID cards.

"Is there anywhere we could talk without being disturbed?" the agent continued. "It is of vital importance to you. Dr. Liebhart sent us here personally."

Liebhart, thought Rawenduzy? The Head of the State Police? Rawenduzy remembered him precisely. They had met during the attack on the OPEC Headquarters. What in the world could Liebhart want with him?

He immediately took the two representatives into the office's kitchen, which also served as a small, private conference room. They were asked to wait – Rawenduzy had a patient, and patients' appointments took priority. With this, the doctor disappeared.

The receptionist served coffee, milk, and a carafe of fresh water, and brought magazines and daily newspapers to help pass the time. The police officers made themselves comfortable.

After about half an hour, Rawenduzy returned. Relaxed, he took a seat across from the men. The elderly couple had cancelled their appointment, so he could devote his full attention to Dr. Liebhart's agents.

"Gentlemen," he said. "I am here. What is so urgent that your boss would send you all the way to my office?" He poured some water and drank it quickly. Although he appeared calm, he actually felt rather uneasy.

"Yes, Doctor," said one of the agents. "I will come straight to the point. The State Police has received a confidential tip off... this is serious... that an attempt on your life has been planned."

"I have known about this for a week," Rawenduzy said, interrupting the police officer. "I also had a confidential tip in this matter."

Surprised, the men leaned forward. "What?" said one of them. "And you are only telling this now?" The other officer lit a cigarette, lost in thought. He took a few puffs, blowing the smoke out through his nose, and then he put out the cigarette. He looked nervous.

"There is nothing I can do about it," Rawenduzy said quietly. After all, who knew of the dangerous methods of the Baghdad regime better than he did? He was well aware that it made no difference to Saddam Hussein if enemies were executed in Iraq or beyond her borders. Iraqi agents would find and eliminate opponents at the farthest reaches of the globe, and most of the time no one would even know it. It would look like an accident.

The two police officers asked Rawenduzy to visit Liebhart in his office the following morning, so they could develop a strategy for protecting the doctor.

The next morning, heavy rain pounded on the windows of the Austrian State Police.

Already 10:00 AM, Liebhart thought, and still so dark. He loved it when the sun beamed its rays into his office, but today there was no chance. With a sigh he was turning back to his files when his secretary announced a visitor – a certain Dr. Rawenduzy.

Liebhart got up and greeted the doctor enthusiastically. They got down to business immediately.

Liebhart explained that the matter was too serious for him to do nothing. Rawenduzy was now a well-known personality, and it was Liebhart's duty to protect him. The Chief of the State Police could not possibly risk harm to Rawenduzy, and if Rawenduzy were provided with around-the-clock police protection, it would thwart any planned attempt on the doctor's life. Liebhart and Rawenduzy concluded the conference by setting up a personal meeting between Rawenduzy and Dr. Erwin Lanc, the Austrian Minister of the Interior.

From that day on, Rawenduzy had a shadow, a shadow made of flesh and blood, a shadow who had completed a special training program for the Vienna Police Corps, a protector whose service to the Republic of Austria was guarding the life of a loyal citizen. The agent's mere presence caused many a comical scene at the doctor's office. Polite patients would insist that this gentleman had been there long before them, and that he simply had to be permitted to see the doctor first. The officer was usually able to explain that he was only holding a seat for his wife. Rawenduzy always had to suppress a smile when he listened to the conversations between his patients and the undercover officer.

Time passed. After three weeks, the scare was over. Kreisky had personally intervened. Diplomatic talks at the highest level between Vienna and Baghdad had guaranteed that there would be no further danger for the prominent Kurd.

During an official reception at the OPEC Headquarters in Vienna, the Ambassador of Iraq in Vienna told Rawenduzy that no attempt on his life had ever been planned. All the same, the next day Rawenduzy received a call from the Chargé d' Affaires of Iraq, a Kurd and the head of the Iraqi Secret Services. He wanted to meet with Rawenduzy. Alone. He wanted to clear the air.

Rawenduzy invited him to his office in Kaisermühlen, and stressed most emphatically that the Iraqi should come without a machine gun.

The discussion ended up being quite calm. They drank strong tea, and Rawenduzy repeated the statements he had made about the Baath regime on the ORF program. The man sitting across from him listened intently; one could only guess what he was thinking. He made no comment, and the two men exchanged little more than small talk before the guest took his leave.

When the representatives of the Austrian State Police heard about this meeting, they quite rightfully reproached Rawenduzy. They had been protecting him and taking care of him. How in the world could he do this?

"I have always told you that I am not afraid," replied Rawenduzy. He offered no other explanation. Fear tortures man. Man becomes constrained by fear. Fear makes a man deny himself. Therefore, fear had no place in the life of Dr. Wiriya Rawenduzy. Not in his earlier days, and certainly not now.

The Road Back Home

In your soil, I am a deep-rooted tree
It is your love that waters me.
O yes, Kurdistan, beautiful homeland,
It's you who created me,
It's you who gave life to me.
That's why Kurdland, my sweetest homeland
I only enjoy life
When I see you happy
and I feel miserable
When I see you in trouble.
Because, Kurdistan, beautiful Kurdistan,
You are my Kaaba,
My belief,
My Yezdan.

DILDAR (YUNIS RAOUF), KURDISH POET (1918–1948)
translated by Omar Dizayee

Dr. Rawenduzy and I worked together at the Austrian Red Cross, so it seems reasonable to devote some space to the Red Cross itself, an international movement and the foremost humanitarian institution in the world.

The history of the organization is well known. The Red Cross was founded by Swiss businessman Henry Dunant in 1859, in Solferino. Dunant created the Red Cross's symbol, a red cross on a white background, by inverting the color scheme of the Swiss flag, which is a white cross on a red background. At the same time as he created the Red Cross, Dunant organized the Geneva Convention, and was awarded the first Nobel Peace Prize for his life's work. Today, there are more than 150 national chapters of the Red Cross and Red Crescent (the name of the organization in the Islamic world, so named because the Islamic half-moon symbol replaces the Christian cross as the organization's symbol).

Thus, worldwide participation in the international Red Cross is high, which would seem to mean that most of the world's nations, as well as their political leaders, have joined in the effort to relieve human suffering. However, the horrible images that TV delivers to our living rooms daily attest to the contrary. Millions still live in pitiful conditions, for many reasons: political power struggles, unimaginable vanity, and economic mega-coups that feign an interest in the common good.

Nevertheless, more than two hundred and fifty million Red Cross workers worldwide, as well as volunteers, work daily to promulgate the philosophy of the Red Cross. They work in war and in peace, and they serve the world's citizens regardless of color, creed, religion, political status, or nationality. They work to embody the seven principles of the Red Cross: humanity, impartiality, neutrality, independence, voluntary service, unity, and universality. These seven principles compose, at least in theory, all that is needed to minimize human suffering. However, they function only as long as the suffering does not exceed the capabilities and resources of the Red Cross.

Dr. Wiriya Rawenduzy was a long-time employee of the Austrian Red Cross, and he understood that the international connections of the Red Cross offered an extraordinary opportunity to help the tormented Kurds of Iraq.

Since 1991, Kurdistan had been suffering from a double blockade. First, there was the embargo of the United Nations against Iraq, which made it difficult to import urgently needed medical equipment and life-sustaining medication. Secondly, the Iraqi government of Baghdad, who considered the Kurds an odious people and had no interest in their welfare, boycotted all shipments to the Kurds. The consequence of these two blockades was an extremely high mortality rate, especially among children.

At this point, it seems appropriate to mention a fact that dismays me, both as a woman in general and specifically a mother. It is a situation that is inconceivable to any Central European with medical insurance and a caring physician.

When I was raising my daughter and she might happen to get sick, we merely had to visit a pediatrician, receive his diagnosis, and then walk down the street to the pharmacy and pick up our medicine. It was routine, and we could do it any day, at any time.

However, in many countries on this planet, people do not have access to such services. They cannot always obtain the medicine they need, at least not officially. And even if they can get it, it costs money. Often a lot of money. Usually too much for the poorest of the poor.

Countries like this do not have public health programs, so individuals cannot benefit from them. The question then becomes, how do mothers cope with the situation? It would seem they must live in a state of endless despair and plight – to have to watch a sick child suffer, knowing they could survive if only they had the needed medication. Often, women offer their bodies in exchange for medicine, in exchange for a box of tablets that in the west are stocked in doctor's cabinets and given away as samples.

When we understand this situation, it is no wonder that Dr. Rawenduzy began to organize relief shipments for the Kurds personally. He collected medicine untiringly. He worked with top-ranking employees of the Austrian Red Cross to set in motion logistics and financing efforts. He was successful. Over the last thirty years, he has been responsible for shipments valued at about one million Euros.

It has not been an easy effort. There is always sluggish bureaucracy in the process, and it causes one complication after another. Sometimes the problems bothered Rawenduzy deeply. At times, he even thought of resigning. Nevertheless, he never gave up.

He did not give up in 1975, when a large portion of a relief shipment from Austria was severely misused by the Iranian Red Crescent. At that time, the Kurds had recently organized a revolt, and the shipments were for Kurdish refugees of the conflict. At that time, the President of the Iranian Red Crescent was the sister of The Shah of Iran, Reza Pahlevi. The Iranian Crescent and its President were responsible for getting the shipment to the refugees, but this never happened. Instead, the entire relief shipment, clothes, blankets, sleeping bags, and more, were sold at a bazaar in Tehran. 1.3 tons of medicine never reached the people for whom it was intended.

Dr. Rawenduzy did not give up on trying to help the Kurds in 1985, when more than fifty cartons of high grade medicines were left rotting in an airport in Paris. In this situation, the medicines simply could not be transported to Iraqi Kurdistan, for reasons that remain obscure. Many tried to intervene on many levels, but it was of no use. The press covered the issue, diplomats worked on the issue, and the Red Cross societies in both France and Austria joined forces and fought to get the shipment to Iraq. However, there were no results, and the losers were the Kurdish people.

Rawenduzy did not even give up later, when Kurdish intermediaries were responsible for the loss of close to 900 kg of medication valued at sixty-three thousand dollars. Rawenduzy personally flew to Istanbul at his own expense, worked with a representative of a renowned pharmaceutical company in Turkey, and was finally able to get the precious freight transported to Kurdistan. Here, however, he encountered more obstacles. A revolt had just begun in the region of Kurdistan bordering Turkey, and this interfered with the Red Cross's plan to dispatch trucks to transport the medicine to Iraqi Kurdistan. Because of the revolt, this plan seemed out of the question. Nevertheless, Rawenduzy and his ally from the pharmaceutical industry used every means at their disposal and succeeded in getting the trucks rolling. However, when the trucks left, there was no Kurdish representative present in Istanbul, nor did Rawenduzy receive any confirmation that the relief shipment had arrived in Zacho, an Iraqi frontier town.

Months passed. Nobody had the slightest idea where the shipment was. Rawenduzy was furious with his people, immeasurably disappointed, and in great internal pain over the whole affair. How could this happen, he wondered? Why had nobody been there at the agreed upon date? Had they not received his faxes? It had taken him three months to plan this operation – three long months: a lot of time, money, and nerves. Of course, Rawenduzy kept things in perspective – he had known true misery, and these frustrations were not true misery. However, it was important to him because he also knew that a small aid shipment that seemed like a drop in a bucket could still save human lives.

It was a disgrace. It seemed that no one had attached any importance to the medicine. Rawenduzy returned to Vienna and began to investigate the matter exactingly, purposefully, and full of bitterness.

Three months later, he received a thank-you note from the Kurdish Ministry of Health. Apparently, the medication had been received in good order. They were greatly obliged to him, and to the Austrian Red Cross.

Nevertheless, Rawenduzy was extremely upset by so much ignorance, and decided to break off all ties with those in charge in his homeland. For seven years, the doctor refused to renew any political contacts. His disappointment was just too deeply rooted.

Then, in January 2000, Rawenduzy received an invitation from Mam Jalal Talabani to visit his native land and renew their friendship. By this time, Rawenduzy had already retired and had left his doctor's office to his son. He was now free of professional responsibilities, but he could not yet make the decision to leave for Kurdistan. What would be waiting for him there? No, somehow he felt the time was not yet ripe to return to his homeland. He politely thanked Talabani, and postponed the trip.

Almost twelve months went by, and Rawenduzy's friends in Kurdistan did not give up. They wanted to welcome Rawenduzy home. They wished to see him in Kurdistan again, and to pay their respects. They also wanted to thank him profoundly. They went to great pains to convince him to come to Kurdistan, but Rawenduzy again declined. Later, he responded once again.

However, fate apparently had other plans. In December of that year, Bahros Galali, a representative of the PUK (Patriotic Union of Kurdistan) in Tehran, paid a surprise visit to the physician. The two men were longtime friends, and as they met, they drank sweet tea, ate yoghurt, and held long discussions. Galali brought interesting news about Kurdish politics and society, and it intensified Rawenduzy's yearning for Kurdistan. At one point, Galali gently patted his friend on the shoulder and said resolutely that he would only return to Kurdistan if Rawenduzy accompanied him. From this point on, Rawenduzy forgot the word 'later'.

He would go, he decided. He would go home. Home, after forty-eight years. His heart filled with deep emotion and unspeakable bliss. For all of the years since his departure, he had repressed so many personal thoughts and feelings. Originally, when he had bidden farewell to his parents, he had only thought he was leaving to go study for some years in a foreign country. He had planned to return to Kurdistan, able to help his people as a qualified physician. However, everything had turned out differently. Soon after his departure, his father had passed away. Likewise, he had never seen his mother again.

Rawenduzy closed his eyes. Oh how he looked forward to traveling to Iraqi Kurdistan. He knew the trip would entail great hardship, but it did not matter. He had already made up his mind.

Galali returned to Iran and arranged an Iranian visa for Rawenduzy. The doctor's itinerary would take him from Vienna to Tehran, and from there he would fly to Kirmanshah, a town near the Iraqi border. Then the trip would continue by car, for hours on end over bumpy roads. By taking this route, one could easily enter Kurdistan.

Rawenduzy had to make various private travel arrangements. His to-do list was long, and Rawenduzy prepared for the trip painstakingly. He did not want to take chances.

Time passed swiftly. At the beginning of March 2001, everything was ready. An Austrian Airlines plane took Rawenduzy from Vienna to Tehran. On the plane, charming flight attendants served aperitifs, and then for the main meal passengers could choose between filet of pike-perch, tomato pulp and Indian corn, or Beef Stroganoff with mashed potatoes. After eating, Rawenduzy leaned back, satisfied, and looked out the window into the dark night. It was a starless night, and the sky had wrapped the silvery plane in a huge, dark-blue blanket. The constant hum of the engine was a never-ending, droning lullaby.

3:00 AM local time. The Tehran airport seemed to slumber. Rawenduzy disembarked from the plane. His friend Bahros Galali awaited him in the arrivals hall, and Rawenduzy greeted him cordially. He retrieved his luggage, and headed toward the exit, pulling the small grey trolley behind him. Cold air chilled their faces. Galali hailed a taxi, and away they went, speeding through the outskirts of Tehran. Soon they arrived at an elegant hotel in the heart of the city, and Rawenduzy had a chance to relax after his long trip. The room would be at his disposal until 9:00 AM, and then Galali would pick him up and take him to the aircraft that would transport him to Kirmanshah.

The room was tastefully arranged. It had a light grey velour carpet that perfectly harmonized with the room's mahogany paneling. Near the window, a flower arrangement accentuated the wallpaper's soft pastel shades. The bed was covered by a fluffy, pale-pink comforter that was already pulled back to reveal bright white linen sheets that made the bed very inviting. The room was a pleasant temperature. Rawenduzy took a long, relaxing shower and dropped off to sleep.

The next morning, when Rawenduzy came downstairs into the lobby, he found Galali leaning back comfortably in one of the hotel's club chairs, and sipping a strong black tea. Galali had already taken care of the formalities at reception, so they were ready to depart. Rawenduzy stole a glance at his watch. It was almost 9:00 AM.

The two-engine propeller plane had a rough landing on the rugged terrain of Kirmanshah. It is a town of almost 250,000 inhabitants in the Iranian part of Kurdistan, and it is the home of a significant cultural asset: Cuneiform, an ancient form of writing approximately 5000 years old, is on display at a museum built especially to highlight the history of this ancient script.

On the road to Iraqi Kurdistan. Border control. March 13, 2001.
The text on the sign says "Welcome to Kurdistan".
Right: Newshirwan Mustafa, the "second man" of the PUK.

Rawenduzy and his companion were met at the airport by representatives of the PUK, and were taken to an elegant hotel. They were told that a two-day stay had been arranged, and that then they would proceed to Iraq by car, as one could not cross the borders every day.

The foyer of the four-star hotel "Azadka" was dark, yet the hotel seemed comfortable. Rawenduzy was tired, and his body needed rest. He discovered an elevator across the hall, which should have been able to take him to his room on the third floor. Unfortunately, it was out of order.

"Damn," he cursed faintly in German. With difficulty, he found a dimly lit stairwell and climbed the stairs to the third floor. The door to his room was made of dark, brown wood, and when he opened it stale air assaulted him. Disgusted, he entered the room, threw open a window, and flung his suitcase into a corner. There was a heavy woolen curtain, and it allowed no fresh air to penetrate the room. Rawenduzy pushed the curtain aside angrily, and took a deep breath.

He looked out over the houses and suddenly felt an intense physical urge grip his innards, and realized that the long trip had thrown his body's clock out of balance. Oh damnation, he thought. He had forgotten that an appropriate toilet was unheard of in this region, even in a four-star hotel.

When Dr. Rawenduzy told me this anecdote, I remembered the words of my father, who worked in Tehran as an engineer in the 1930's. He spent approximately twelve months there. When I was a child and I would pick at my food and refuse to eat it, he would smilingly tell me that when he worked in Tehran one of his staple foods had been yellow, strong-smelling mutton butter. He had eaten this for an entire year.

Two days later, Rawenduzy and Galali journeyed by car into Iraq. After two hours on the road, the small group crossed the border.

There were no incidents. When the visitors were announced, it was a mere formality to check their passports and admit them to Iraq. That check point was only open two days a week, and even on those days it was only passable for a few hours.

"Welcome to Kurdistan!" trumpeted a large green sign with black Arabic letters and Kurdish words. This sign was the first thing to greet Kurdistan's lost son when he entered the country. Before Rawenduzy could comprehend that he had finally arrived in his homeland, another surprise greeted him. A delegation of high-ranking Kurds were waiting for him on the other side of the border to welcome him home. Among them were Talabani's nephew, Schirwan Mustafa, the deputy head of the PUK, as well as the Director of the Ministry of Health, Dr. Hama Khoshnaw.

The group was overjoyed to see Rawenduzy; tears of joy were shed, and these same tears dried unnoticed as the old compatriots greeted each other. What a cordial reception, marveled Rawenduzy. What a warm-hearted welcome, even after half a century. Deep satisfaction filled Rawenduzy's heart, and he stepped into a comfortable limousine.

For a few seconds Rawenduzy paused and tried to turn back the clock. Had it really been nearly fifty years? Vienna had certainly become his new home, but should he not more truly call it his second home? He certainly had enjoyed living in Austria, but he had to acknowledge that he had irrefutable feelings that rooted him in Kurdistan.

Acknowledge, he thought. Had he never acknowledged these feelings? There had been neither time nor space for personal confessions. Since he had arrived in Austria, he had been immersed in the perpetual motion of human existence, a daily struggle that had been at times a heavy burden. In all that time he had never had the luxury of allowing sentimentality to take over.

The two-hour car ride brought them to the impressive home of the Hafid family in Sulaymania. The owner, a well-known lawyer, had also come to the border and had invited the entire welcome committee to dine at his house to honor his special guest. Kurdish hospitality is well-known, even beyond the borders of Iraq. At this feast, food was served in abundance, the sheer variety of dishes demonstrating the importance of the people present.

Several hours later, after he had thanked the woman of the house, Rawenduzy was taken back to his hotel in the center of Sulaymania. He was then assigned two bodyguards, who were heavily armed and would be responsible for his safety day and night.

The hotel room, which included both a bath and a toilet, was very comfortable, and Rawenduzy was relieved to get rid of his tight shoes. He reflected on the last several hours, and realized with surprise that he was no longer used to the cordiality and openness that was so common here. He was also now unaccustomed to his homeland's cuisine. Slightly weary, he stretched out on the sofa and closed his eyes.

He had had only a few minutes to relax before there was a knock at the door. One of the bodyguards poked his head in and announced with a trembling moustache that Mam Jalal Talabani had arrived. He and his entourage were already in the hall downstairs, along with journalists and a television team.

"You are expected, Boss," he concluded to Rawenduzy.

His tone was urgent, and it made Rawenduzy hurry. He got up quickly, forced his tired feet into his narrow shoes, and rushed downstairs.

He was very late. The television broadcast was already in full progress, and suddenly Rawenduzy realized that he was not dressed according to etiquette. He had forgotten a jacket and tie. Luckily, he had a friendly, almost brotherly relationship to Talabani, and since Rawenduzy was a VIP, people seemed to overlook his discourtesy generously. Nevertheless, he was embarrassed – after all, the same rules of etiquette applied to Central Europe as to Iraqi Kurdistan.

Several hours later, his bodyguard asked him discretely if it was now fashionable in Europe to dress casually for official functions. Rawenduzy thought he would die of shame. He was worried by his misconduct and extremely annoyed with himself. What unforgivable neglect on his part, he thought. How could he possibly have let this happen?

During his trip to Iraqi Kurdistan Dr. Rawenduzy faced his own past and tried to come to terms with the present situation in Iraqi Kurdistan. Both the political importance and human drama of this trip should be described in this chapter, but to do so exhaustively would be beyond the scope of the book. Therefore, in accordance with Dr. Rawenduzy's wishes, I would like to restrict myself to a brief sketch of the visit.

It was a tight schedule. There were state banquets. There were political discussions meant to promote and hasten reconciliation between the conflicting Kurdish factions. There were press conferences and live television interviews, as well as guest lectures at the Sulaymania University Medical School. There were visits to the hospitals and uncountable glasses of tea with friends.

Rawenduzy discovered that the attack on the OPEC Headquarters in Vienna was still drawing media attention in the Middle East, even after so many years. One incident highlighted this. During Rawenduzy's visit, several Arab journalists, among them a correspondent of the Arabic daily "Al-Sharq", and a journalist from the Kuwaiti newspaper "Al-Anbaa", asked Rawenduzy to describe the horrific event in detail. Their discussion lasted for several hours, and during the interview Rawenduzy learned that Al-Nakasch was living in Tehran, and that a meeting between the terrorist and Rawenduzy could easily be arranged. Rawenduzy declined. What would have been the use of such a confrontation?

Rawenduzy's visit was in the middle of March, and it coincided with the commemoration of the attack on Halabja. Halabja is a small provincial town, approximately 260 kilo-

With PUK Chief Talabani (right) and Ing. Saadi Dizayee, Minister of Building. March 13, 2001.

Reception in Hotel Ashti. Right: Ing. Galali

meters north of Baghdad and eleven kilometers from the Iranian border. It has lush vegetation and it is the site of the Darbandikhan reservoir, these two factors allowing the Kurdish population to engage in animal husbandry and sheep breeding. Years before the events that would later make Halabja famous, a group of warriors had banded together in Halabja and the surrounding villages such as Kormal and Dojeyleh, and together they had fought fiercely against the never-ending assaults of the Iraqi government.

Friday, March 18, 1988:

The horizon is brightly lit by the first rays of sunshine. In the distance can be heard the muffled roars of aircraft engines, and despite the early morning hours, Halabja is already bustling with activity. Many people are already out and about in the city, and some children have already begun to play in the street in front of their houses. It is Friday, and the simple, modest life of these rural people seems to be taking its normal course. The only abnormal thing is the roar of airplanes, which seems to draw closer and closer each moment. What could this mean? Worried, some of the inhabitants of Halabja begin to search the sky.

Today is Jabar's birthday. He is twelve years old, and is extremely proud that he is now allowed to help his father at work. Jabar is the oldest son of the Duqany family. At the moment he is diligently stacking the heavy wooden planks his father will later use to make tables and chairs in his meagerly-equipped carpenter's shop. His three brothers run noisily back and forth between the street and the house, begging Jabar to play with them. Outside, the six-year-old Goli, Jabar's only sister, is busy feeding the chickens. She is followed by a small dog that constantly jumps into the air, attempting to snatch the chickens' breadcrumbs from Goli's hands.

Jabar places the last wooden plank on the wobbly rack. Satisfied, he inspects his work. Now his father can start cutting the wood. Quickly, he wipes his brow on his sleeve. Today is a special day, and in Jabar's honor there will be sweet cakes. Jabar is overcome by a feeling of happiness. But what is that noise outside? It is deafening.

Meanwhile, Iraqi fighter jets approach the Kurdish town of Halabja. They are loaded with a deadly payload – poison gas, produced in Iraqi factories and officially designated pesticides. The pilots of the airplanes reach the town and fly low over the houses, dropping bombs filled with the chemicals. Repeatedly the planes roar over the town. The air raid is brutal, and does not seem to end.

The order to attack Halabja was the work of one Ali Hassan al-Majid, an Iraqi general who considered the ethnic cleansing of the Kurds to be the foremost mission of his political existence. His orders were to be precisely and perfectly executed – Ali was the cousin of the Iraqi dictator Saddam Hussein, and the pilots of the planes knew that if they did not carry out their orders properly, they would be executed.

By the time the people of Halabja and the surrounding villages recognize the danger it is already too late. Escape is impossible.

Suddenly, Jabar feels a burning sensation in his throat. He tries to swallow, and succeeds only with excruciating pain. His skin burns as if on fire. There! He sees Goli! Goli, he cries! But his cry to his sister is choked. His sister lies on the ground, gasping to her dog, which lies lifeless at her side. A tremor runs through her body for the last time, and the look of desperation on her face freezes forever.

Allah, have mercy, cries Jabar to himself. His three brothers have collapsed at the house's front door. Their mother must have tried to help them shortly before her death; her badly burnt arms now embrace the inanimate bodies of her sons.

Father, beloved father, please help me, cries Jabar! There is another explosion, and the stillness that follows is pierced by

Over 10,000 Kurdish poison gas victims in a hospital.

March 18, 1988, after the poison gas attack on Halabja.

Gravestones in Halabja.

screams. The air is filled with yellow clouds of dust, obscuring vision, and there is a foul stench. It seems the world is ending.

Jabar wants to run away, but his legs give out and he falls down. With his last bit of strength, he struggles to get up, but fails. His small fingers clutch the ground, and he feels a stabbing pain in his chest.

"I am suffocating," he whispers. "Suffocating..."

The boy becomes unconscious, and soon his weak breath stops. In a moment, his heart ceases to beat.

Jabar means "powerful". Under Saddam Hussein's rule, power dominated law. Ali Hassan al-Majid, later known as "Chemical Ali", exercised a demonic power. He hated the Kurds passionately.

The brutal massacre in Halabja would go down in history as "Bloody Friday". The results were gruesome. More than 5000 people were killed, among them many women and children who died an agonizing death. More than 10,000 people were severely injured, many of whom died later as a result of their wounds. The rest of the people fled, their houses razed to the ground by Saddam Hussein's troops, who followed in the wake of the warplanes.

Since the attack, Halabja has become a symbol of the Iraqi regime's war against Iraq's own people. Physicians, both Kurdish and foreign, have examined the attack's survivors, and have documented an astonishing array of diseases, including but not limited to nerve damage, cancer, osteomyelitis, severe birth defects, sterility, and psychological maladies.

Furthermore, the assault on Halabja of May 18, 1988 should not be thought of as an isolated case. Roughly 4,500 settlements were destroyed in the campaign, and close to 200,000 people were abducted and murdered in Kurdish northern Iraq. It was nothing less than mass murder, ordered by the Iraqi government and carried out by the dictator's assassins. Mass murder, only a few hours from the greedy hearts of the west and the financial moguls of Eastern Europe.

Dr. Rawenduzy's commemorative journey to Halabja affected him deeply, and he could neither comprehend it nor digest it. His stomach and intestines revolted. As a physician for internal medicine he attributed the problem to the region's rich cuisine, which was no longer normal for him, but even a mind as clear as his could not negate such deep psychic wounds as he found in Halabja. Only time would assist in quieting these thoughts.

In addition to his official appointments, Rawenduzy wished to visit his birthplace, the town of Rawenduz, today a small provincial town of 5,000 inhabitants. For a long time this town was the historic center of the Kurdish people. For 650 years, it had been the seat of the Kurdish Suran dynasty. In the first half of the nineteenth century, under Muhammed Pasha Kor, the town of Rawenduzy achieved remarkable significance because Kor succeeded not only in uniting large

Dr. Rawenduzy was born in Rawenduz in Iraq. This small town was destroyed and set on fire by the Russians several times!

portions of Kurdistan, but also in producing the country's first cannons. To commemorate this achievement, a cannon has graced the entrance to Rawenduz ever since.

In addition to his birthplace, Dr. Rawenduzy's journey back home also took him to Erbil, probably the oldest town on earth, and once the religious center of the Assyrian culture. In Sumerian, the town was known as Urbilem. The oldest parts of the castle of Erbil consist of 506 apartments, most of which have been declared officially protected historical sites.

At the time of Rawenduzy's visit, Erbil was also the seat of power of Massoud Barzani, a politician who governed the northwest region of Iraqi Kurdistan and was Mam Jalal Talabani's opponent. Everyone knew that if Barzani and Talabani were to unify, it would end a decade-long civil war among the Kurds. The result would be a unified Kurdistan that could stand against the Iraqi government and make a heroic push towards autonomy. The basic problem of the Kurds has always been their internal quarrels. The legendary general, Mustafa Barzani, Massoud's father, had been able to win popular acceptance of the concept of Kurdish unity, but it lasted for only a short time and immediately after Mulla Mustafa Barzani's death, the Kurdish political leadership split.

Both sides held fast to the general goal of "Azadi bo Kurdistan", freedom for Kurdistan, but no one could agree as to how it should be accomplished. The Barzani party, the Democratic Party of Kurdistan (DPK), formerly the KPD (Kurdish Democratic Party), made up one side, and the Patriotic Union of Kurdistan (PUK), Talabani's left-wing movement, founded in 1976, was the other side. Talabani's group demanded, among other things, a joint Iraqi resolution that would include both Kurds and Arabs.

Rawenduzy made an attempt to influence these critical and urgent matters. He was on friendly terms with both Barzani and Talabani, and in a personal discussion with Barzani he emphatically pointed out the political benefits of a union between the two parties.

Unfortunately, in the midst of these trying times, news was received of the assassination of Franswa Hariri, one of Barzani's closest associates. Hariri traveled with six bodyguards, but somehow assassins had succeeded in shooting him in the Bazaar of Erbil. It was another attempt to rekindle the seemingly endless fighting of Kurd against Kurd.

After intense investigations by the police, as well as numerous arrests, it was quickly discovered who was behind the attack, and the guilty parties were taken into custody immediately. They proudly claimed to be followers of the terror group "Ansar al-Islam", a branch of the notorious Al-Qaeda. About a hundred followers of Ansar al-Islam had taken up headquarters in the nearby villages of Biyara and Tawela. Both were close to Halabja and adjacent to the Iranian border. Relieved, Rawenduzy continued on his journey, pleased that Barzani had pro-

With Massoud Barzani. Barzan. March 23, 2001.

mised to continue negotiations with Talabani without restriction, and that he would retain as the primary goal of the negotiations the establishment of a free and united Kurdistan whose people would fight together for their national rights.

The remaining days passed at breakneck speed, and were filled with countless impressions. On March 21, while Dr. Rawenduzy was in Sulaymania, he and his companions celebrated the Kurdish national holiday. The festival is called Nawros, and it is the anniversary of the Kurds' liberation from a barbarous ruler named Dehokor al Dahark, whose legendary excesses occurred more than 2500 years ago. According to the Kurdish calendar, it was the year 2616, which equates to our year 2004. At the celebration of Nawros, bonfires are lit as a symbol of liberation, and the people sing and dance. All troubles are temporarily swept aside, and the Kurds connect with their roots and take a moment to feel the Kurdish blood running through their veins.

Here it is worth discussing the position of Kurdish women. In contrast with other Arab nations, Kurdish women are emancipated and take an active part in public life. Kurdish women have equal rights under the law, and consequently can hold important positions, positions that, in other Arab countries, are normally reserved for men. The attire of Kurdish women is fashionable, even by European standards. The kerchief and veil that most Arab women must wear are unimaginable.

In addition, Kurdish women's organizations have long since succeeded in having polygamy, the Islamic tradition under which a man can marry up to four wives, abolished. In addition, a Kurdish woman can obtain a divorce by herself with a court order, something unheard of in the Arab world, and in Iraqi Kurdistan a woman who is unfaithful to her husband may not be punished with acts of violence. In former times, amorous escapades were often repaid with death.

Unfortunately, violence against women is still a sad subject, a subject ignored by many states. Nevertheless, the Kurds of Iraq have made efforts to improve things in this area; for example, to protect battered women and their children, three shelters were opened in Sulyamania, all of which are supported by public funds.

In addition, illiteracy poses a great problem in Kurdistan. Nearly 50 percent of Iraqi Kurds can neither read nor write. Two thirds of these are women. For these women, a logical step towards independence is to take evening classes. In particular, rural parts of Kurdistan have high illiteracy rates, so schools in villages often offer classes for free. In this way, Kurdish women of all ages are given an opportunity to overcome the serious shortcomings of their situation. It goes without saying that Kurdish men are also allowed to participate in such night courses.

The health system in Kurdistan is still woefully lacking. The physicians are hindered by antiquated equipment and unavailable medicine. Nevertheless, public confidence in hospitals has increased, largely because of mothers-to-be, who have begun to choose to give birth to their babies in hospitals rather than at home, which is often complicated. Furthermore, for the well-being of male babies, circumcision is now only performed by doctors, and then primarily in hospitals.

Kurdish women in Iraq demonstrate not only inner sublimity but also outer grace. They have suffered the pain of wars and terrorist attacks. They have lost innumerable husbands and sons. They have given their strength to the Kurds' never-ending fight for freedom, while trying to make a peaceful contribution to world history, both present and future.

The day Rawenduzy had to bid farewell to Kurdistan was a sad day for him. He thanked his hosts and voiced a strong intention to return soon. His heart was filled with enormous gratitude for Galali, who had been a faithful friend along his "road back home". After 48 years, here was a beginning. He now knew that he, as a son of Saladin, would return to his homeland. He would return to a united Iraqi Kurdistan, defiantly showing a bold face to Saddam Hussein and his regime's atrocities. He, Dr. Wiriya Rawenduzy, would return to his Kurdistan, a Kurdistan that dreamed of a democratic future and believed it had a realistic chance to realize this dream, regardless of how many obstacles remained.

Terrorism and the Cancerous Development of World Politics: From Bruno Kreisky to George W. Bush

Throughout human history, people have tried to gain power by force. Whether we consider the French Revolution's Reign of Terror, or more recently Germany's Rote Armee Fraktion, we find that all such movements have a common denominator – the systematic use of terror to attain military, political, or even social objectives.

In recent history, the extent of terrorism has expanded internationally because of a terror organization known as Al-Qaeda, which has managed to incorporate many autonomous splinter groups into their logistical base (Al-Qaeda, roughly translated, means 'base'). However, these terrorist splinter groups have lost sight of their original goals. Whether they use the Islamic religion to try to camouflage their aims, or they simply and nakedly use violence to achieve power, their objectives are obvious: to demonstrate their strength in order to spread panic and fear. Their foremost goal is the destruction of human life, which shows that humanity, humanity's dignity, and the common bond between all people, has become meaningless to terrorists.

The Viennese philosopher Erich Heintel, who was greatly influenced by Immanuel Kant, formulated the following moral imperative, which attributes rationality to human existence. This moral imperative applies to the whole of the human experience:

"Act according to what is humanly essential to you, and respect your fellow-man beyond his nature as an individual – respect him for his humanity."

There is more to a human being than his membership in the animal kingdom, or than his species. A man is a man because he practices humanity. This distinguishes man from all other animals, who have to live out their lives within the confines of their species. They cannot help this; they are born this way. However, man is different. Although men look alike on the outside, they do not necessarily all live humanely. A man becomes a true human being only when he works on himself and follows his mission without making excuses based on his role in society.

Another key point in Heintel's philosophy is that when a man acts selflessly under great duress, which in the worst case could mean the sacrifice of his own life, he becomes a true human being. To put it simply, if a man does not demonstrate humanity, he merely lives within the confines of his species and is no more than an animal.

In a democratic constitutional state, the country should be governed by the dignity of man. In some constitutions, this goal is clearly defined, and hence mandatory. The goal is achieved in various ways, but the most important way is through legislation. Through legislation, states attempt to achieve a sensible system and good social conditions.

If we consider this, however, we find that it exposes a limit to the state's power. Specifically, if the state is based on conscience, and on the dignity of man, the state has a permanent responsibility towards human conscience and dignity. This can create problems. For example, some citizens, based on their conscience and human dignity, choose not to comply with their national duty to bear arms. These citizens are called conscientious objectors. In addition, even when citizens do obey the law, their obedience can be triggered by conscience and morality, but also by any of the other reasons, people obey the law.

Politics boils down to power, power executed by rulers, and this raw power lies at the heart of every government, regardless of how the governing parties came to be in control. Even so, many different forms of government have existed since time immemorial, and still exist today. However, they do not all protect and support human dignity equally, no matter what they may claim. This is the situation today.

If we track the political developments relating to the gain and loss of power, we find that there are two kinds of leaders: those who use power to gain more power, and those who serve humanity and human dignity. In addition, history has shown us many instances in which these two motives are mixed, and many examples in which all leaders claim to serve humanity and dignity, and blame violations of human dignity on their enemies. Therefore, justice and injustice can be distributed quite unevenly.

In the first type of leadership structure, that which uses power to gain more power, leaders seek to preserve and increase their power. In a milder form, leaders favor privileged groups and try to protect them. This type of power must of necessity lead to hypocrisy and deceit. It expects the ruled to keep the rulers in power, even if the rulers arbitrarily suppress and exploit the ruled. Another common facet of this form of leadership is propaganda, a means by which the ruler seeks to "keep them stupid", and to use any problematic information or opinions for their own purposes.

Politics is extremely important; an individual cannot escape the fate of the state and society into which he has been born. Therefore, political action is the bull's eye of freedom, something of the utmost significance in world history.

As we strive to think politically, we must take into consideration the nature of the nation-state. The nation-state alone can declare war and make peace. This makes the nation-state the true unit of political action. Thus, although the world has come to be united in trade and cultural exchange, civilization still faces insoluble issues because the problems of today run up against the conflicts in interest of nation-states. This makes it difficult or impossible to overcome the stark contrast in abundance and deprivation we see in the world, as well as the alarming level of shortage and starvation. It is clear that the problems of the civilized world cannot easily be solved economically, nor can they likely be solved without risking the environment, because doing so would overstep the bounds of the nation-state.

Numerous international institutions have been created, and even now, they are working, more or less successfully according to their goals, to establish a system of international peace without which a dignified society is impossible. These international institutions encounter many difficulties, but there is no other way given the conflicting demands and politics of nation-states.

As we have already seen, the most important ways nations tackle political problems is through legislation. After this, the judiciary and police forces regulate the problems of society that inevitably occur when people live with other people. Thus, legislation is an instrument of sovereign authority. However, it should not serve merely to maintain power – it should serve humanity.

Humanity-centered legislation is still just legislation, but it also remains long after it is enacted, as a statement of guiding principles. This is important because human relations are multi-layered, and in any society, justice is rarely practiced as well as it could be, or as well as we would like. Nevertheless, there should always be a strong positive argument present in the public sphere, and humanity-centered legislation provides this argument. It should be common language in a society that legislation may have only one goal – to preserve the dignity of the individual and to help him develop his liberty.

When we consider the essence of law, we find two possible inherent tensions. The first is the tension that arises when each person is out only for himself and hence must contend with a world of others who are out only for themselves. The second tension is the tension that results when one tries to find a common ground between his own liberty and the liberty of others, an effort which is difficult because the process is as important as the goal – the common ground must not only be found, but it must be found with justice and dignity.

It would be naive to deny that behind law and its effectiveness there is power. It is not enough in the legislative arena to call for understanding, to make appeals to conscience, not even if the ideas we espouse are engrained in the conscience of the citizens. Eventually legislative efforts that ignore power will be doomed. History supports this observation. Repeatedly, in many ways, often under the guise of conscience, man has risen against existing legislation, even if society supports it.

An extreme and dangerous example of this is terrorism. Terrorists regularly claim that they are impelled to act by conscience, guided by morality, and intent on creating a better society. However, the means by which they seek to achieve their ends betray their stated goals and motivations: they use naked violence, and violence is something that people, through legislation, have long since rejected as an acceptable means of accomplishing anything.

A walk through history shows that terrorists have existed since time immemorial. In approximately 1100 BC, Pharaoh Ramses III ruled Egypt's twentieth dynasty. A papyrus dated to the reign of his successor outlines a case dealing with a conspiracy. Today, historians believe that the conspiracy was against Ramses, and that the Pharaoh lost his life in the plot against him.

There are numerous examples of this in history, ranging from the murder of tyrants to assassinations that instigated desired changes in world history. All of these examples clearly demonstrate the belief of terrorists that killing is justified if it supports their politics and ideology.

In the last century, a new breed of political murder has appeared – international terrorism. It is different from previous forms of terrorism because it can strike anyone, anywhere in the world, at any time, and it causes enormous suffering among citizens. In Europe, the ETA (a Basque terrorist group which aims to separate the Basque provinces from Spain), and the IRA (Irish Republican Army, which seeks to separate Northern Ireland from Britain), have drawn the Spanish and Irish into merciless maelstroms of bloodshed and hatred.

In the 1970's and 1980's, Germany and other nations were shaken by left-wing extremism and left-wing terrorism. The young, middle-class generation of the post-war period began to cast a critical eye on the government and the post-war years of "Wirtschaftswunder", Economic Miracle. The protestors adopted as their slogan the phrase "Terror on Consumption", and began a campaign of arson in department stores. Soon they followed with demonstrations and street fights, targeting the Alex Springer Publishing House and installations of the US Armed Forces. Eventually, they even managed to murder several high-ranking state officials.

In May 1970, Andreas Baader was forcefully freed from prison in Berlin, and under his leadership the RAF (Rote Armee Fraktion) came into being. Ulrike Meinhof was also instrumental in this assault, and as a result of her participation the RAF was often referred to as the Baader-Meinhof Group. The members of the RAF were been trained in a military camp designed for radical Palestinians, and when they returned to West Germany, they terrorized the entire nation. They saw themselves as fighting a battle against imperialism, and they fought their battle with precision, abandon, and indescribably brutality. They committed violence against other human beings, and they knew no boundaries in doing it.

The RAF called for a nationwide war against the system, a call that was met with no response from the German government. Nevertheless, the German people grew enraged with the RAF, and soon they even began to demand the death penalty for terrorists. Finally, in the 1970's, the police succeeded in arresting the leaders of the RAF.

In the recent past, right-wing extremism has increased, along with all of its cruelty. Both in Europe and in the United States, right-wing terrorist groups target foreigners, minorities, refugees, homosexuals, and even the handicapped. They follow the example of Adolf Hitler, basing their ideology on nationalistic, radical, and neo-Nazi principles.

In these groups, self-appointed leaders often lure young people into the fold by using their discontent to inspire hatred. They preach that democracy is impotent, and they lead their followers into solutions of violence against the perceived guilty parties, such as foreigners, homosexuals, and left-wing intellectuals. Members of such right-wing movements undergo mandatory weapons training and combat exercises, and they often desecrate graves, usually those in Jewish cemeteries. In their line of thinking, it is completely normal to burn down foreigners' living quarters, sometimes even when the occupants are inside.

The first assault by a radical right-wing group after World War II occurred on September 26, 1980, and resulted in the deaths of thirteen people. In this assault, a right-wing radical detonated a pipe bomb at the main entrance of Munich's Oktoberfest. The total casualties amounted to thirteen dead and 211 injured, 68 of them in serious condition.

Nor was Austria free of political extremism. One year after the OPEC attack, the German terrorist Bock was arrested in Vienna. In response, the RAF assassinated numerous people in order to force his release, but their efforts were unsuccessful. The RAF was also responsible for the abduction of a tycoon named Palmers. He was released for an enormous ransom. In this case the abductors were eventually caught. In addition, in the mid-nineties, two left-wing extremists attempted to blow up a high voltage mast in Lower Austria. The attempt was unsuccessful, and both perpetrators lost their lives.

Open right-wing extremism ended after World War II, but it began to resurface after Austria was freed from occupation by its State Treaty. Various national youth organizations and sporting clubs were founded, and many of them had political leanings. During a crisis in South Tyrol, right-wing extremists appeared in great numbers and executed several explosions. A man named Norbert Burger founded the National Democratic Party (NDP), became notorious, and then saw the party dissolved for good in 1988. Nevertheless, radical splinter groups mushroomed, and their neo-Nazi activities eventually surpassed those of the NDP. A wave of arrests followed; nevertheless, bombs, even letter bombs, often claimed civilian victims.

On February 4, 1995, activities of right-wing extremist groups reached a highpoint when four Roma (gypsies) perished in a bomb attack near a Roma settlement in Oberwart, Burgenland. In 1999, Franz Fuchs was found guilty of the crime. He committed suicide in his cell.

Arab terror first caught the eye of the world more than a half century ago. In May 1948, the state of Israel was founded, an event which triggered a volcanic political explosion in the Middle East that has endangered world peace ever since. The problem is that two groups of people live in the region – the Israelis and the Palestinians. The Palestinians have been living there for centuries, the Israelis lived there centuries ago and intermittently since then. The two groups now fight for one land, formerly known as Palestine, each side claiming it for themselves according to their own interpretations of history.

Tension mounted quickly in Israel as both sides began to use greater and greater force. Soon approximately a million Palestinians had to flee the region.

The Israelis, strengthened by aid from the United States of America, have relentlessly continued their occupation. The government of Israel employs an inhumane and brutal settlement policy in occupied areas. Thus, the territory that actually belongs to the Palestinians has become more and more a part of Israel.

The expelled Palestinians live with hate, rage, and a sense of powerlessness. Generations have languished in overcrowded refugee camps without any hope for a better future. The political and social injustice of the situation provides the basis for constant radicalism. Fanaticism blooms in Palestine, and violence has been on the rise ever since Israel was established. There have been various peace negotiations, but the situation has remained largely the same. Now Palestinians continue to demand a state of their own, just as they always have.

The Palestinians' leader, Yasser Arafat, publicly condemned acts of terrorism twenty years ago. Nevertheless, radical factions of the Arafat's group, the Palestinian Liberation Organization (PLO), have continued to carry out suicide assaults, and in recent years, the number of attacks has multiplied. The Israeli army reacted barbarously to these assaults, destroying many cities in the autonomous Palestinian regions, and murdering many civilians.

By now, the world seems to have adjusted to a state of permanent conflict in the Middle East. The United Nations attempts to solve the conflict, but their efforts are to no avail. As a result, the public normally focuses on the Islamic fundamentalists and forgets that there are also fundamentalist tendencies within Christianity. What, then, is the common denominator in all this?

First, the followers of such fundamentalist groups obey orders blindly, without deliberation, fanatically heeding the leaders' orders and simple messages. These orders disregard tolerance towards people of different faiths or opinions. Thus, these groups create enemies for themselves, enemies who must then be fought, even with violence. Such groups hold harsh, seemingly patriotic beliefs; promote strict, sometimes bizarre morals; and affirm the death penalty as a basic operating principle. They also tend to suppress women – women and men are generally not equal for them – and they usually forbid basic school instruction on human sexuality and reproduction.

In the United States of America, television has allowed fundamentalist Christians to reach a mass audience. They have achieved enormous success over the airwaves, through a combination of demagogical skills, rhetorical training, and perfectly staged manipulation of the masses. Amazed and uncritical, many Americans accept the sanctimony that fundamentalists present as fact, firmly believing and supporting these preachers with generous donations. The logical consequence of this is that politics are influenced as well.

In Islamic countries, different criteria create the basis for fundamentalism. Desperate people turn to fundamentalist leaders because the masses are impoverished, unemployment abounds, and there are few structured training programs. Iran is a good example of this, and it is useful to note that the fundamentalist government of the Ayatollahs could not solve Iran's problems.

Many Arabian and African countries have fundamentalist governments, and in all of these countries, we see that the people are suppressed. In particular, female members of the population are punished harshly for disregarding the traditional Islamic dress code. Each time a fundamentalist regime takes action against the people it is justified by religion. In Arab countries, the life of the individual is determined by religion. According to the Islamic Scharia law, governments may punish citizens with stoning, amputation of limbs, public flogging, torture, and more. Islamic regimes forever promote the refusal of western political systems, culture, and economic structures. If citizens do not comply with the wishes of fundamentalist regimes, they are punished severely and without exception.

Until recently, the center of Islamic fundamentalism was the Taliban, the former government of Afghanistan. In Afghanistan, Osama bin Laden, Islamic extremist and founder of the terror organization known as Al-Qaeda, found the perfect place to set up the base of his worldwide terror organization.

Bin Laden's name has been on everyone's lips since the terrorist attacks of September 11, 2001. He is supposed to have been instrumental in the attacks. But who is Osama bin Laden, this man said to be the most evil man on the planet?

Osama bin Muhammed bin Awad bin Laden was born in 1957 in Saudi Arabia to a Syrian mother and a Yemenite father. His father was immensely wealthy, and is said to have had ten wives, four primary wives and six secondary ones. Osama is likely the seventeenth child of fifty-seven. The bin Laden family is one of the richest families in Saudi Arabia outside of the royal family. In addition, they have excellent connections with the Saudi royals, and this helped Osama's father become a billionaire with his construction and transport company. Osama studied economics in Jeddah.

In April 1978, a democratic party in Afghanistan stood up for reforms such as strengthening farmers' and unions' rights, separating church and state, establishing equality for women, and improving the school system. This party favored strong ties with the Soviet Union and consequently broke off ties with rich Muslim landowners. As a result, under the guise of defending Islam, the rich landowners began to fight against progress. The United States of America, which dreaded any increase in power by the Soviet Union, subsequently began to support the Afghanistan Mudschaheddin, the former rich landowners, now turned fundamentalists.

In order to prevent the overthrow of the new and progressive Afghani government, the Soviet Union sent thousands of Soviet soldiers to Afghanistan. For more than ten years, the USA, other western governments, and wealthy Saudi Arabians supported the fundamentalist Mudschaheddin. Across

Afghanistan sounded a national battle cry, a cry for liberation. The cry was "jihad", Holy War.

It seems that in those days the USA was concerned not only with the retreat of the Soviet Union from Afghanistan, but also with promoting the spread of Islamic fundamentalism to the Central Asian Republics of the Soviet Union. The intent was to trigger a smoldering, unstable process that would weaken the Soviet system.

Osama bin Laden, a millionaire and hence a man of independent means, left Saudi Arabia in 1979 to fight against the Soviet invasion of Afghanistan. Trained by the CIA and supported by immense sums of US money, he founded an organization known as Maktab al-Khidmat. Under bin Laden's leadership an estimated 30,000 soldiers or more were enlisted from foreign countries, trained, drilled, and financed in Afghanistan. In addition, the CIA secretly delivered arms and military equipment to Afghanistan. Reliable reports also state that the Americans trained the Mudschaheddin in "everyday terrorism", such as the use of car bombs in attacks against the Soviets.

After the conflict in Afghanistan, bin Laden returned to Saudi Arabia and soon separated from the Wahabites (Sunni Muslims – the royal family of Saudi Arabia come from the Wahabitan line). Soon thereafter Iraqi troops marched into Kuwait and the United States sent approximately half a million soldiers into Saudi Arabia to contest Saddam Hussein and the Iraqis. Osama bin Laden opposed this move, causing Washington to designate bin Laden a terrorist.

Eventually the Gulf War ended, but American soldiers remained in Saudi Arabia. This caused bin Laden's anger to boil over. He let it be known that in his opinion his homeland, as well as Egypt and other Middle Eastern states, were nothing but US puppets. The Saudi royal family responded quickly to bin Laden's counter-governmental activities, and soon he was stripped of his Saudi Arabian citizenship and exiled. Later his family would disinherit him.

Osama bin Laden left for Sudan. At first, because of his wealth, the Sudanese government accepted him with open arms, but eventually they yielded to US pressure and exiled him just as the Saudis had. Bin Laden then returned to Afghanistan, began once again to set up training camps, and offered his services as well as the services of thousands of fanatical mercenaries to the fundamentalist Taliban regime. This time the Holy War would be directed at the USA.

Bin Laden was the first Muslim to officially oppose the Americans, and he came to be seen as an intellectual representative of the radical Islamic movement and the ideology underlying it. He became a role model for many Muslims. It was easy for anyone to identify him; he became their figurehead. His goal was simple – to drive the Americans from Islamic territory, and to destroy the state of Israel. The ends would justify the means, even if the ends were the murder of innocent people.

The list of terrorist attacks perpetrated by bin Laden and his people is long, including thousands killed and even more injured. In 1998, bin Laden's organization attacked the American embassies in Kenya and Tanzania, for the first time creating an international stir. On March 11, 2004, a terror attack in Madrid exposed an Achilles heel in Europe: 191 people perished and more than 200 were wounded or seriously injured in explosive blasts on four overcrowded commuter trains.

After the attacks on the World Trade Center and the Pentagon on September 11, 2001, attacks in which more than 3000 were reported dead, people began to grasp the reality of the new wave of terrorism. It was a phenomenon that had developed in the last decade of the twentieth century and was no longer restricted to any region or area.

In the seventies and eighties, international terrorism seems to have differed in structure from modern-day terrorism because modern terrorism is more global and more capable of unified action. The present day terror network covers the entire world and allows decentralized collaboration between friendly terror groups and cells. Therefore, leaders can plan and execute parallel operations at the same time in different parts of the world. This network has enormous financial resources, both legal and illegal, and it brings together people from around the world, people with diverse national, cultural, linguistic, and ethnic backgrounds. The basis of the network is joint subversive action in favor of Islam. The network supplies the logistical support, and the organization's ultimate goal is the destruction of the existing international order.

In Iraq, terrorists today are individual commandos who often work autonomously and seem to have lost site of sequential steps. They have become machines of death, filled with hatred and conducting a dirty war against everyone and everything. Since the overthrow of Saddam Hussein, the terror scene in Iraq remains diffuse, and cannot be compared with the situation in the greater Middle East. Prior to his downfall, the dictator pardoned some thousand criminals who had been sentenced to death for their crimes. After April 10, 2003, the elite Baath party teamed up with these ex-criminal commandos. In addition, terrorist groups had infiltrated Iraq from neighboring countries in order to prevent Iraq from stabilizing.

Currently, Saddamites, Wahabites, and Islamites are fighting against the Americans and their allies. Megalomania, lust for power, and the hopes of future sovereignty over the entire globe make them believe unconditionally in their cause. The Wahabites come predominantly from Saudi Arabia and have interpreted Islam and the Koran to have prophesized a coming world Islamic supremacy. The Wahabitan terrorists demonstrate an incredible destructive capacity, a capacity that probably stems from their religious background and has been demonstrated in numerous attacks in Saudi Arabia.

When the Afghani Taliban regime lost power in December 2001, Al-Qaeda was also beset with difficulties. Large portions of their training and communication capabilities were probably lost, and as a result, much of their base withdrew to Northern Iraq. As already mentioned, the villages of Biyara and Tawela, both a few kilometers from the Iranian border, were considered strongholds of Islamic fundamentalism.

Among the Kurds, one also finds supporters of Ansar al-Islam, a joint organization of Al-Qaeda and the Taliban. Mullah Bachtiar, an Iraqi Kurd, is in close contact with the Jordanian Abu Massab Al Sarkawi. He is the leader of Ansar al-Islam, a terror group that trains suicide commandos for their bloody plans.

Since the overthrow of Saddam Hussein, violence has ruled in Iraq. In addition, there have been attacks in Kurdistan and they continue to this day, not only against American troops and their allies, but also against the party offices of the PUK and KDP in Erbil. Hundreds have been killed and a large number injured. The assassination of Hariri, a confidant of Barzani, and the possible consequences of that assassination for the Kurds, have been discussed in a previous chapter.

If one were to casually survey the daily world press, he would observe a persistent international phenomenon – the suicide assassin. At the beginning of the eighties, suicide terrorism took place in Lebanon and Kuwait. Lebanese Islamic fundamentalists had their new methods confirmed when they used a suicide assassin to attack a US Marine Corps post, and the Marines were subsequently ordered to leave Lebanon. This success elated Islamic groups. Although Islam, just as Christianity, considers suicide a sin, Muslim dignitaries could not prevent suicide attacks, and although the authorities disapproved of the new methods, popular opinion within terrorist groups grew not only to tolerate these living bombs, but to respect and even honor them.

Historians believe the origins of the suicide attack stem from the first half of the twentieth century, when Japanese

Kamikaze pilots in World War II became a serious threat in aerial warfare. Towards the end of the war, the National Socialists (Nazis) used this method in Germany as well. In a last rebellious effort against the enemy, German Kamikaze pilots plunged to their deaths.

Self-destruction with the intent of causing death continued in the Korean War. In the Middle East crisis, the wave of suicide attacks saw its first climax when Palestinian fundamentalists incorporated this terror weapon into their program. The second Intifada, caused by Ariel Sharon and his politics in recent years, made it difficult for many otherwise moderate Palestinian groups to extinguish the blazing flame of suicide assassins.

Different factors motivate a person to become a living bomb. Generally, these people do not speak of killing themselves, but rather of sacrificing themselves in the name of Allah and Islam, the only true belief. Secondly, suicide bombers are assured that they will be famous after they are dead, that they will be honored as martyrs, and that their family will be shown enormous respect. According to a recent study, one eighth of Palestinian ten-year-olds wish to die a martyr. They believe, first of all, that when they die they will immediately go to paradise, where they will live for eternity. Secondly, they believe that they are fighting against a superior enemy, and thirdly they believe that to die as a martyr would make them special, each one a person who stands out from the anonymous masses because of his heroic deeds.

These human weapons pose no risk to the leaders of international terrorism because suicide bombers do not have to be protected as they execute their mission, and they do not have to be provided retreat or escape strategies. Furthermore, a suicide assassin can easily adapt his attack to cope with any last minute changes. For those who seek to combat suicide attacks, the threat is constantly present and trained units cannot always prevent them no matter how hard they try. This results in precise acts of terror, attacks that result in immense material damage and horrific harm to innocent civilians, including psychological scars and emotional trauma. The media contributes to the problem because they give credit to the backers of such attacks, assuring that the perpetrators receive the worldwide attention they desire.

Many more or less famous experts have investigated the social background of the suicide assassin and have come to two divergent conclusions.

Conclusion One: Most terror organizations systematically recruit the assassins from Koranic schools, using various selection procedures. These organizations use brainwashing and religious indoctrination to build the basis for future operations. The assassins themselves come from lower social classes, have extremely low financial means, and display evidence of low self-esteem. For them the thought of dying for Allah and securing an eternal life in Paradise seems to justify the self-sacrifice.

Conclusion Two: This model believes less in the religiously motivated, lower-class theory, instead focusing on the educated people of the middle class. Experts believe these assassins are equipped with great efficiency and motivation, are scientifically and technically trained, and come from stable families. They are not forced to join militant Islamic groups by psychopaths, nor by poverty, nor by despair, nor by virtue of having being outsiders. Instead, they join terrorist groups because they have strong beliefs that the world must be changed. They dream of heroism, even as they are being psychologically manipulated.

Analyzing these two conclusions, one thing becomes obvious. If it were only financial need that fed militant Islamic fundamentalist groups, the problem could be solved through economic growth. Unfortunately, this is not the case, as we can demonstrate by observing militant groups in Kuwait, where the per capita income is equal to western standards.

Clearly, wealth does not immunize one against radicalism, and poverty alone does not create Islamic extremists.

Of course, the views of people who are drawn to Islamic fundamentalism could be changed, but it would take the support of leading intellectual Muslims, along with a lot of time. Indeed, it would even be possible to eventually turn radical terrorists into lone assassins, assassins whose actions would prove ineffective in the end; however, this could only be achieved through a cohesive worldwide political strategy, through justice and solidarity, and by constructively dealing with the religious, cultural, and political realities of Islam. This might sound like a Utopian view, and perhaps it is. Unfortunately, the point is moot: there is no room for Utopia in this power-hungry game of world politics, and as a result, we are hopeless against the cancerous growth of terrorism, completely at the mercy of its lethal effects.

Finally yet importantly, we will make an attempt in this chapter to clarify a widespread prejudice that exists throughout the western world. This is the prejudice against Islam, a prejudice shared by many Christians, although normally it is not openly acknowledged. Day in and day out, the news media reports on atrocities and terror attacks perpetrated by Islamic fundamentalists. These reports are passed on around the globe by commentators and reporters, and often they do not do justice to Islam. The viewer or reader can often unintentionally develop a latent aggression towards Islam, an aggression that can lead to serious conflicts with Muslims.

In Austria, the vilification of Islam and its representatives reached a highpoint recently when a reactionary Catholic priest made a negative public statement about Muslims and their religion. Such verbal attacks must not happen. They display excessive dogmatism and contribute to dissent and obduracy. It makes one embarrassed to be a Catholic. A Christian should have the constant desire to treat people of different faiths with love, awe, respect, and understanding.

Most people have trouble understanding Islam because they rarely have contact with Islam's basic principles. In Austria, people have little access to true Islamic culture and religion, and because they have no contact with Islam, they have trouble conceiving that they might share any basic principles with Muslims. As a result, Western thinking often automatically equates Islam with terrorism. Several Islamic regimes have also contributed to this misconception by propagating radical nonsense.

A glance at the past shows how dignitaries of the Christian church have abused power, often mercilessly subjugating and exploiting people. It is clear that religion must be free from power, and authority must be independent of religion.

In summary, our existence should be governed by an effort to attain genuine humanity. Only this will ensure dignity for man, both in his thoughts and deeds.

THE NEW ORDER

For decades, Saddam Hussein and Iraq were two fixed points firmly engrained in Europeans' conceptions of the twentieth century. However, very little was known about the dictator. Of course, school history lessons dealt with the history of the region; it is one of the most fascinating histories on the planet. However, when we compare, for example, the mysteries of ancient cultures with those of modern Iraq, we find the two have nothing in common.

At the end of World War I, after the collapse of the Ottoman Empire, a British mandate established the Kingdom of Iraq. Unfortunately, the constitutional monarchy of the new country inherited almost insurmountable problems, predominantly ethnic and religious disputes between Arabs, Kurds, Turks, Shi'ites, and Sunnis.

In 1932, Iraq became independent, and was accepted into the League of Nations. At the end of the 1950's, internal political instability rocked Iraq, and as a result the military gained power. This led to many revolts and uprisings. The monarchy ceased to exist, and a republic was proclaimed. This was the first step towards the unavoidable, tragic fate of Iraq.

Representatives of the ASBP (the Arab Socialist Baath Party, which originated in Syria) were already at work underground. Their chairman was Michel Aflak, a Christian history teacher, and their secretary general was Salah-al-Din Al-Bitar, a Sunni Muslim and physics teacher. Both had studied at the Sorbonne in Paris and viewed their party as an arm of Arab nationalism, a region-wide movement that promoted general government control of trade and industry, with slight exceptions that would allow modest private industry. The movement also worked for changes in the social, ethnic, and religious structures.

In accordance with these views, the party also promoted "Arab Rebirth" for most minorities (the word "baath" means rebirth). After the Baath party seized power in Syria, it split into two factions: the anti-Marxist civil faction, and the military-dominated faction. In the ensuing power struggle, the military faction triumphed, and Michel Aflak, leader of the civil faction, was exiled. Aflak took refuge with Saddam Hussein in Iraq, eventually dying in Baghdad in 1989.

Syrian students took over the ideology of the Baath party and spread it to Baghdad. There was another military uprising, and the representatives of the ASBP came to power, beginning to show their true faces by employing violence and brutality. Among other things, members of the Communist Party were executed, and the General of the Army was murdered.

By 1968 the name Saddam Hussein el-Takriti, Deputy Secretary General of the Baath party, had already appeared on the political horizons of Baghdad. Saddam Hussein cared nothing about the ideals of the Baathists or their efforts to promote equality. His sole goal was attaining absolute power.

The wave of terror continued. The regime persecuted officers, communists, civil servants, and more. Death sentences were announced on television to intimidate the already-frightened population, followed by swift public hangings.

In July 1979, Saddam Hussein took over the Baath party. In accordance with his interpretation of the needs of the moment, all positions in the state were united in one office, his. Saddam Hussein became President, Chairman of the Revolutionary Council, Commander-in-Chief of the Iraqi Army, and General Secretary of the Baath party.

Who is Saddam Hussein el-Takriti? He was born on April 28, 1937, in Ouja, near the town of Tikrit. His relatives were peasant farmers, and he grew up without a father. Biographers give different accounts of Saddam's education. It seems he never finished high school in Iraq, but later completed his training in Egypt. He began to study law in Cairo, and in 1968, after many interruptions, he finally took his final exams. This was, however, only after the successful coup, a coup he co-initiated.

An established fact is that when he was a young man he was intensely interested in the biographies of Babylonian Kings and Arab Rulers. He took a great interest in the career of Nasser, the Egyptian President who rose to power in Cairo in 1952 and was hailed as the Pan-Arab leader in Iraq. Historians and psychologists believe that Saddam Hussein's political aggression had already come to the fore when he was still a young man. In 1957, he joined the extreme, violent Baath party, and started a conspiracy against then-Prime Minister General Qassim. The conspiracy was unsuccessful.

During the assassination attempt on Qassim, Saddam Hussein was injured. He managed to escape, first to Syria and then to Cairo. In 1960, while he was out of the country, the Iraqi government sentenced him to death.

Later, four years after Qassim was overthrown, Saddam Hussein returned to Baghdad, and was immediately given a higher position within the Baath party, that of Head of Security Services. In his new position he was often reproached, which indicates that he might have been part of an internal power struggle. In any case, he was arrested in 1963. After his release from prison, he went underground.

However, his period of hiding was brief. By 1968, Saddam Hussein belonged to a group of Baath activists who were responsible for the overthrow of President Abdul Rahman Arif. The new President, Ahmed Hassan al-Bakr, a man from Tikrit who was said to be a relative of Saddam, was installed, and Saddam Hussein was appointed Deputy Secretary General of the Baath party.

Immediately, he began to organize his own secret service. What did this mean in practice? Hussein had non-Baathists fired from all government and military posts. He intimidated his own people, and formed a special "Revenge Corps" to prevent any rivalry. From this point on, torture and capital punishment were the order of the day. Hussein persecuted not only political dissenters, but also his own personal political opponents, specifically Kurds, Communists, Shi'ites, Jews, and others.

The Kurds, who are not Arabs, repeatedly demanded autonomy from the Baghdad government, and attempted to enforce their requests through revolt, revolts that ended in bloody suppression. In 1970, the Kurdish Democratic Party under General Mulla Mustafa Barzani signed a peace treaty with Saddam Hussein's revolutionary commandos. However, appearances were deceptive; the regime in Baghdad had signed the peace treaty only to buy time.

Two years later, in 1974, Saddam Hussein began to nationalize western oil companies, who until them had had a monopoly on Iraqi crude oil. Consequently, Iraq rose to a new and highly significant position in the Arab world and around the globe. The economy of Iraq started to boom. Raw material and machinery were purchased, as were weapons. In Saddam Hussein's opinion, the Kurds were still a problem. It was decided that General Barzani should be deposed, but an assassination attempt failed. In addition, the Kurdish Peshmergas, equipped by Israel and Iran with war equipment and food, fought the Iraqi troops fiercely, and the regime's army suffered much bloodshed. This was considered the climax of Kurdish militancy.

Surprisingly, the archenemies Iran and Iraq settled their border conflicts in March 1975. Iraq relinquished disputed territory at the Schatt al-Arab River, and in return, the Shah had the borders closed and withdrew support for the Kurds. In June of 1975, the leaders of both countries signed this friendly agreement between two neighboring states.

The losers were the Kurds. Their resistance was crushed, and Saddam Hussein was provided the opportunity to satisfy his mean streak. Without any protection from the Peshmergas, the Kurdish civilian population was at the mercy of the Iraqi army. The Iraqis devastated Kurdish villages, forced the resettlement of hundreds of thousands of Kurds to the south of the country, and destroyed the structures of Kurdish inhabitation and crop cultivation.

In the following years of his dictatorship, Saddam Hussein steadily maintained his campaign to turn Kurdish land in Iraq into Arab territory, and he did it without regard for human rights conventions. He forcibly deported the Kurds from the town of Kirkuk, intending this to serve as an example and a warning for all. Arabs settled in Kirkuk, and more than half a million Kurds lost their property and had to flee to the mountains.

The year 1979 was a decisive one for Saddam Hussein. President al-Bakr resigned, and Saddam Hussein was sworn in as Head of State. In addition, he conferred upon himself the leadership of the Baath party, the only party with any power in Iraq.

But how did the dictator actually succeed in gaining such a firm grip on all positions of power, and how did he maintain this firm grip for decades? This is a tricky question, a question with many layers and much diversity, a question that requires several answers.

Saddam Hussein's brutal power structure was based on two key elements: family/clan thinking, and police state/party structure. Hussein filled key positions in the state, in industry, in the secret service, and in the army with half-brothers, cousins, and other loyal relatives. The Tikrit clan expanded by marriage and developed a family and tribal empire, an empire that became immensely rich through oil money. Family members could afford any conceivable luxury, and were therefore completely devoted to the dictator. However, if any member of this widespread family network aroused even the slightest suspicion of disloyalty, even if the suspicion were unfounded, he paid for it with his life.

Moreover, Saddam did not order murders merely of his family. Two of his sons-in-law, both high-ranking military officers, were murdered after they and their families left Iraq for Jordan. Saddam's daughters, Rana and Raghad, saved their own lives by divorcing their husbands.

This net of authority was primarily controlled by two of Saddam's sons, Uday and Qusay, who also acted as their father's presumed successors. Saddam's first choice for a successor was Uday, who displayed atrocious brutality and little intelligence. Reports of rape surfaced almost daily, and one day, without provocation, he struck and killed one of Saddam Hussein's tasters with a wooden club. Uday was in charge of youth organizations, which acted as militia federations. He also screened the country's media.

After Uday was seriously injured in an assassination attempt, his younger brother Qusay became first in the line of succession. Qusay was more intelligent and much more disciplined than his brother was, and he took responsibility for the Secret Service. Because of him, thousands of political prisoners were murdered.

Both brothers ran profitable smuggling operations, trading in petroleum, cigarettes, alcohol, automobiles, and foreign currency. Their smuggling efforts, which the UN sanctions against Iraq made possible, generated an annual profit of approximately $ 2 billion for the two men.

Saddam Hussein never made a secret of the fact that he had his political opponents murdered by the thousands. He seemed to be proud to be known as the strong man of Iraq, a leader who ruled his country with an iron fist. He fought internal wars against rebellious Kurds and Shi'ites, wars that strengthened his lust for power and allowed him to arbitrarily decide between life and death for his enemies. He ordered the draining of the swamps of Southern Iraq, swamps that were the livelihood of the Shi'ites who lived there, and soon after, he began a systematic attempt to exterminate the Shi'ites.

Saddam Hussein had his own interpretation of who was and was not an Iraqi citizen, an in accordance with his interpretations he expelled from Iraq approximately 500,000 Faily Kurds, people who were born in Iraq and held Iraqi citizenship but were somehow classified by Saddam Hussein as Iranians.

Saddam Hussein used terror in many forms to maintain and increase his power. These forms included but were not limited to a corrupt police state, an informant network, denouncement, a large secret service, and twisted political ties within the Baath party.

In 1990 and 1991, the Baath party systematically began to lose members, due to Kurdish revolts in the North and Shi'ite revolts in the south. Saddam Hussein first decided to deal with the situation by carrying out a bloodbath among his enemies, and then by beginning a propaganda campaign designed to show Iraq his fervent belief in Islam. Soon pictures of the dictator praying at a mosque were everywhere. Perhaps wishing to go down in history, he ordered statues of himself erected throughout the land, and he sought to portray himself as a Babylonian ruler who wanted to establish a new era of Arab glory. He considered himself a successor to the Prophet Muhammad. Soon paintings of Saddam Hussein fighting against infidels decorated innumerable buildings.

We see the real Saddam Hussein when we consider his fanatical megalomania and his unwavering lack of character, even towards his allies. In spite of the peace agreement with Iran, in 1980 Iraqi troops invaded Iran. The historic feud between the two nations had been rekindled anew, and the conflict would later go down in history as the first Gulf War.

In 1979, after the overthrow of the Shah in Iran, the revolutionary leader Ayatollah Khomeini took over the reigns of power. Soon after, Saddam Hussein attacked Iran. The west supplied Iraq with the necessary weapons, and from 1987 on, tens of thousands of Kurds were either expelled from Iraq or killed by the despot's Special Forces, all of this under the cover of war.

The bitter conflict with Iran did not bring victory. In 1988, the opponents signed a truce. Eight years of continual war had resulted in roughly two million dead and injured, as well as a financial disaster for Baghdad. All of the nation's monetary reserves had been spent, and Iraq had incurred an additional fifty billion dollars in debt. Each day the army became a source of insecurity for the dictator, and the party steadily lost control of large areas of the country.

In August of 1990, Saddam Hussein annexed the rich Sheikdom of Kuwait, and proclaimed the occupied territory to be the nineteenth province of Iraq. He did this to improve Iraq's financial situation. However, the Iraqi army's defeat was inevitable. An international military alliance under the leadership of the United States of America launched "Operation Desert Fox" and put an end to the aggressor's plans. Cornered, Saddam Hussein ordered the oil fields of Kuwait to be set on fire, causing an ecological catastrophe. At the same time, Iraqi troops withdrew, as did the troops of George Bush senior.

Because of Iraq's defeat in the second Gulf War, Baghdad was forced to accept the resolutions of the United Nations, which included the payment of war reparations, the abandonment of weapons of mass destruction (WMD), the admission of weapons inspectors into Iraq, and more. These resolutions were to be strictly observed, and in order to safeguard the Kurds and Shi'ites the Allied Powers erected protective regions and no-fly zones. The tyrant Saddam Hussein remained in power, and despite alleged covert efforts by the CIA, he was not overthrown.

The world took an ambivalent attitude towards Saddam Hussein, especially groups with vested economic interest. Above all, the weapons lobby had to guarantee that their dirty business could continue. Lucrative profits could be made by transferring technology to Arab countries. Moreover, Saddam Hussein succeeded once again in making silent arrangements with leading politicians from many states around the globe. In the meantime, Iraqis suffered in servitude under his authoritarian rule.

The Iraqi population had to endure more and more. Because of the continuing UN sanctions, the economic situation in Iraq steadily worsened. The people, unable to resist the regime, fell into abject poverty and despair, and daily survival became next to impossible. The United Nations "Oil for Food" aid program did not ease the tense situation. Despite the plight of the Iraqi people, however, the dictator continued to have magnificent palaces built for himself. It is worth mentioning here that foreign companies also conducted profitable business.

After 1991, democratic structures began to develop in the autonomous Kurdish areas, but the political split that occurred there seriously hampered them. The Kurdish leaders Massoud Barzani and Jalal Talabani emphasized to the foreign press that although they saw the right to autonomy as the unquestionable basis for any new state structure, they had no intention of separating from Iraq. Nevertheless, Turkey continued to threaten the Iraqi Kurds.

The example of Iraqi Kurdistan highlights the difficult position of anyone who opposed Saddam Hussein. On one hand, Saddam's opponents knew that the Kurds could only be liberated from Iraq with the help of the West, specifically with the help of the United States of America and Great Britain. In addition, one could never peacefully reform the regime in Baghdad; an overthrow had to be forced from the outside. Any opposition, therefore, had to rely on those who had previously wanted to free Iraq from such outside influence.

Meetings between representatives of opposing Iraqi parties took place in major foreign cities and in the Kurdish city of Salah-Uldin. They came from the many tribal opponents of the regime in Baghdad – Arabs, Kurds, Turks, and more – and they had a single goal: to dispose of the tyrant and his followers.

An abundance of mineral oil and natural gas can be a blessing or a curse. Other states craved the mineral resources of Iraq, and their craving grew daily. The United States of America, who had significant petroleum reserves themselves, headed the group of nations who were interested in Iraqi oil. For some years, the US had been reducing the amount of oil it imported from Saudi Arabia because the US government did not trust the politically unstable Saudi regime. From the American point of view, if America wished secure its energy resources in time to meet future demands it was necessary to depend on alternate suppliers. The USA uses roughly one forth of the world's fossil fuel, yet considers it superfluous to cooperate responsibly in a worldwide policy of climate protection.

After the election of President George W. Bush, whose father had already been at war with Saddam Hussein but had decided for tactical and precautionary reasons not to overthrow the dictator, the American oil industry came closer to a goal that had formerly seemed unattainable: the revenue of the second largest crude oil reserve in the world, the mineral oil of Iraq.

George W. Bush's closest associates have well-known connections in the oil industry, forming a wheel of power. This is not surprising, as the President himself once worked as a manager among the oil barons. The goal of gaining control of Iraqi oil had to be attained, and making it come true was critical for world politics. However, the image that the United States uses force only for clean purposes was not to be tarnished.

9/11 gave Bush a reason to declare war on terrorism. At first this war was met with approval in many Muslim states, and internationally as well. Al-Qaeda was centered primarily in Afghanistan among the Taliban, so the Bush administration and its allies planned to remove both the terrorist cells and the Taliban regime in a single campaign. In the course of this war uranium ammunition was used, and Afghani citizens sustained deplorably heavy losses.

Meanwhile, the Bush administration was already preparing for the next war. In his State of the Union address at the beginning of 2002, Bush referred to North Korea, Iran, and Iraq as an "Axis of Evil". He maintained that "states like these and their terrorist allies constitute an axis of evil aiming to threaten the peace of the world." The President had already accused Saddam Hussein of having an atomic weapons program, as well as weapons of mass destruction. The head of the International Atomic Energy Commission stated Bush's accusations to be unjustified. Many UN weapons inspectors had not been able to find any sign of weapons of mass destruction, and until now they still have not. In his speech, Bush offered several other official speculations:

1. Iraq has connections to Al-Qaeda.
2. The weapons of mass destruction are hidden in Saddam's palaces, to which UN inspectors are denied access.
3. The USA has proof that weapons of mass destruction do exist.
4. A change in regime is absolutely necessary.
5. Iraq must be democratized.

Furthermore, guided by his deep belief in the Almighty, Bush felt he was personally called upon to destroy evil in this world.

The UN National Security Council did not issue the USA a mandate to go to war in Iraq. Opposition to the US's plan ran high, and even the Pope warned against the war and the terrible consequences to which it could lead.

Nevertheless, the USA formed a coalition with several states. In February of 2003, millions of people around the globe participated in anti-war demonstrations, even in countries who had pledged their solidarity to Bush.

Regardless of the opposition to the war, everything proceeded as Bush and his people had planned long before. In a dramatic speech, George W. Bush announced the war on Iraq. On March 20, 2003, heavy bombardment began, and soon Iraq capitulated. The administration in Washington had promised a short and "humane" war. Selected US journalists reported live from the theater of operations, but all commentary had to be approved by the military and signed by Armed Forces authorities.

The Iraqis put up fierce resistance against the invaders. The bombs of the so-called liberators often hit residential areas and killed innocent civilians. In the Arab world, hatred for the US mounted, and Arabs declared their solidarity with the dictator. In a statement completely bereft of good taste, US Secretary of Defense Donald Rumsfeld cynically referred to the war in Iraq as an "act of humanity".

The downfall of the Saddam regime in Baghdad ended the third Gulf War. Anarchic conditions prevailed. Armed gangs stalked the streets and began to loot the city. The water and electricity supply broke down, hospitals were closed, and hospital patients were left to fend for themselves. The risk of an epidemic skyrocketed.

Saddam Hussein had disappeared. The population seemed elated by the liberation. The US military conducted further attacks. Even after the official end of the war US soldiers continued to fall victim to attacks, and frustration began to spread among US forces.

For more than a year, the US forces tried with every military means at their disposal to get Iraq under control, but each day American soldiers died in acts of sabotage or in bomb attacks. Iraq remained a cauldron of trouble not only for the occupying forces but also for foreigners and Iraqi citizens who collaborated with the "aliens". In addition, religious groups formerly hostile to each other now found they had something in common – Islam – and united against the occupying forces.

Terrorism could neither be defeated nor wiped out in Iraq. Experts are now of the opinion that the actions of the USA in Iraq actually encouraged international terrorism. According to a United Nations survey, under American occupation Iraq has become the central arena of Al-Qaeda and all of its splinter groups.

On December 14, 2003, Saddam Hussein was captured and subsequently displayed in the world media in ways designed to strip him of any appearance of authority. Unfortunately, however, Saddam's capture has not helped to stabilize Iraq. The incidents at Abu-Ghraib emphasize the postwar violence. Torture increased within the prison, and US soldiers sexually humiliated Iraqi prisoners.

The governing council installed by the US occupiers had little true competence and no say at all in the use of the oil reserves. A government from outside had been forced on Iraqis again. The struggle to end the occupation grew daily. For any nation, an occupation means a loss of identity, and sometimes even a loss of dignity.

Because of the constant violence in Iraq, an Iraqi interim government took power on June 28, 2004. Occupation by the Allied powers had officially come to and end. The US civil administration, headed by Paul Bremer, was ended.

Success of the new government in establishing democracy will depend on steadfastness and the will to stick it out, as well as on political ability and strong cooperation between foreign armed forces and the new Iraqi government. First, the Iraqi population wants peace and order. The new Prime Minister of Iraq, Iyad Allawi, announced harsh action, and has even spoken of martial law. President Ghazi al-Yawer promised a free and united Iraq, with a full guarantee of sovereignty. A strong military and police force would leave criminals and murderers no chance.

Yawer is said to be an independent and respectable intellectual who takes sides in no party. His appearance is marked by white headgear and a long gown. He has not been afraid to criticize publicly the faulty US security policies in Iraq. In addition, as an Iraqi he advocates a sensible approach which would have the new government break its agreement with the foreign troops in Iraq and determine independently when the occupants must withdraw.

Allawi, on the other hand, is said to have had strong former contacts with the CIA and with the British Secret Service. In spite of this, he presided over the Security Council installed by Paul Bremer and most strongly condemned the brutal actions of the Allied troops in Fallujah. At that time, as a sign of his political and human indignation, he resigned from the Security Council.

In former times, Allawi was a member of the Baath party. However, he could not identify with the bizarre way Saddam Hussein interpreted party ideology. Instead of working for Saddam, he went into exile in the mid-seventies and founded the opposition group al-Wifak al-Watani, which means "national harmony". All Iraqi groups recognize Allawi as a trustworthy politician of consent. Consequently, prominent Shi'ites, Sunnis, and six Kurds are found on his governing team.

The Kurds in Iraq are considered extremely pro-American. It was the Peshmerga, in collaboration with the US military, who discovered the hated despot Saddam Hussein in an eight-foot deep "spider hole", which had supposedly served as his hiding place for months. After he was discovered, his capture was routine. At that time, the United States and its coalition forces urgently needed the triumph of apprehending the most wanted tyrant in the world – it helped them to justify the war. Forgotten was the missing UN Security Council resolution, which should have been necessary to go to war in the first place. The capture of Saddam Hussein also helped Bush to polish up his tarnished image in his own country. The American public had begun to grumble loudly, doubting the purpose of the war. Americans had been receiving daily news reports on losses of American soldiers in Iraq, and this dramatically reduced Bush's approval ratings. After all, the President had to think of the next election.

When the first photos of a tattered Saddam Hussein were released and shown on television around the globe, the Iraqi public was jubilant. The former tyrant had to open his mouth in front of the cameras so a sample of his saliva could be taken for DNA analysis. The authorities wanted to make sure that they had not caught a Saddam Hussein double. Yet even for those who lack psychological knowledge, the reasons for reporting the capture this way are clear – the authorities wanted to degrade and humiliate the man.

This statement should not give the reader the impression that I feel solidarity with such a cruel violator of human rights as Saddam Hussein, or even that I possess an understanding for this barbarous commander-in-chief. Nothing could be further from the truth. It just seems that the US, always so adamant about their humanitarian and moral ethics, could have exercised a somewhat more sympathetic transfer of information.

To return to the Kurds, in the north of Iraq the Kurds came under the protection of the US military, and were able to maintain autonomy in a rather arbitrarily-selected and limited region. As allies of the so-called liberators, they hoped that this autonomy would be extended. However, a UN resolution of June 8, 2004, which stipulated which rights the Kurds had gained, or more accurately had not gained, enraged the leadership of both Kurdish parties. In addition to being denied the rights they had hoped for, the Kurds were completely ignored in the selection of both Head of State and Prime Minister.

The Kurdish leadership voiced their discontent in a letter to President Bush, while in Iraqi Kurdistan protests and petitions were filed. The Kurds were not willing to be treated like second-class citizens, and they were determined to officially secure their rights. For decades, Saddam had carried out a program of genocide, and the Kurds wanted legislation that would end once and for all the possibility of such an atrocity ever happening again. The Kurds did not wish to rely on the promises of Arabs or on political reassurances.

At the UN Security Council, Arabs argued that Islamic rights should be the basis for the fundamental laws of Iraq. This argument was successful, and in Article 61/C of the interim constitution of Iraq, a constitution which is still valid today, the rights of the Kurds are stipulated, stipulations that are expected to hold in Iraq's future constitution.

As a result, in July 2004 more than five hundred intellectuals took to the streets in Sulaymania. The tenor of the large demonstration was clearly defined, and it was clear that the powers that be, both foreign and domestic, should not underestimate the Kurds' determination. If the Kurds' demands were not upheld, the people of Iraqi Kurdistan would stand up for a sovereign state of their own, and they would do it using every means at their disposal. They were not willing to bend beneath the Arab yoke any longer.

For a while, it was anyone's guess as to whether the conflict would again mean war. It would have been wrong to draw the conclusion that the Kurds would now engage in warmongering or would behave aggressively. The Kurds had been consistently and systematically deprived of their own state. To this history can easily attest. Because of this, they understand the treacherous danger of making political promises and then not keeping them. In spite of numerous revolts, thousands of deaths, expulsion, and attempted extermination, the Kurds have never given up on their constant struggle for justice. However, their wish remains – that the policies of the new millennium will help this peace-loving people to overcome the atrocities of the past.

In order to correctly make a new beginning, a different contingency had to be employed, one true to the intentions of the Kurdish people.

The Direct Approach

In the summer of 2002, Jalal Talabani designated Dr. Wiriya Rawenduzy the new Health Commissioner of Iraqi Kurdistan. After his appointment, Rawenduzy originally intended to return immediately to Sulaymania and resume his mission of mercy and his educational efforts. However, personal matters and health problems prevented him from leaving. He had to postpone his trip due to the war in Iraq, due to the occupation and destabilization of the country, due to the Islamic fundamentalist groups, and also because of an urgent and complicated eye operation.

Rawenduzy is an expert in Kurdish affairs, and continues to observe the course of political development in Kurdistan. In June 2004, he met his friend Mam Jalal Talabani in Ankara. Rawenduzy asked Talabani for an interview for this book, emphasizing the significance of the work and its relevance to contemporary history.

Born in Koisanjak in 1933, Mam Jalal Talabani represents an important part of modern Kurdish history. The Talabanis are a large family spread across Iraq. They have become prosperous and respected landowners. They also gained political influence under the British, a development that displeased the rival Barzani clan and resulted in a power struggle that continued at political levels for decades to come. Neither of the two groups wanted to give up their claim to leadership.

As a trained lawyer and the head of the PUK, Talabani positioned his party as a unifying front that would incorporate all of the progressive trends of the Kurdish national movements in Iraq. Their aim was always to create a social system within which there was the chance for the Kurds to realize their dreams of autonomy, including the possibility of forming a state of their own should they choose to.

Today Talabani not only holds the office of Secretary General of the PUK, but also demonstrates his voice internationally. He has been a state guest of President Bush at the White House and is a valued partner-in-dialogue of many European politicians. He has clear ideas regarding the future of Iraqi Kurdistan, and believes that Kurds need to resolve their almost impossible differences by employing models of federalism and autonomy. He points to many nations in Europe that have done so – Belgium, Switzerland, Great Britain, and more. Talabani also cites Canada as an example of what is possible. He feels it is essential for Kurds to work with Iraqi leaders to create a democratic constitutional state that is grounded in the principle of the peaceful and harmonious co-existence of different countries.

In essence, the Arab-Islamic world has to detach itself systematically from all remaining dictators. Arab nationalism must end, as must radicalism towards smaller nations.

The next question points to the trial that Iraqis now eagerly await, and the expected subsequent conviction of Saddam Hussein. Should the former dictator be condemned to death for his former crimes? What is Talabani's point of view?

The PUK leader describes Saddam as an abominable war criminal, a despot comparable only to Hitler and Mussolini. In addition, Saddam has committed crimes without precedent in human history. As his first example, Talabani names the use of chemical weapons against his own people, people who were Saddam's subjects. Secondly, Talabani reminds us of Saddam Hussein's mass graves, in which Saddam's deputies hurriedly buried hundreds of thousands of people. Talabani's indictment against Saddam is quite exhaustive.

There is no doubt in the mind of the PUK Secretary General that Saddam Hussein deserves the maximum possible sentence for his atrocities, but as a lawyer and a defender of human rights, Talabani is strictly against capital punishment, and will not contradict his convictions. He points out that for Saddam Hussein execution would be quick, and the dictator's death would last only a moment, but life imprisonment would give the convict plenty of time to think. The former despot, a man who lived his life possessed by a lust for power, would have to watch from prison as Iraq changed for the better. Talabani believes that it would be more painful for Saddam to watch the progress and prosperity of the country since his political overthrow than it would be to die. However, Talabani stresses that it is not his place to predict the decision of the Iraqi court, since only the court can pronounce the ultimate sentence on Saddam.

The interim government of Iraq reinstated capital punishment, and Talabani was rumored to have objected to it. This, however, is untrue. On the contrary, Talabani is of the opinion that interim government's action will help fight terrorism and capital crime.

Until now, there has been no success in establishing a uniform Kurdish government, so this interview should also address Talabani's position on the separation of Iraqi Kurdistan. How great were the differences between Talabani and Massoud Barzani, son of the legendary leader Mulla Mustafa Barzani and leader of the DPK? Will free elections be possible for the entire Kurdish territory?

Talabani responded frankly to this delicate question, stating that his relationship with Kak Barzani (Brother Barzani) were extremely good. They were working diligently towards their common goal, but Talabani stressed that there must be a smooth transition when it is time to fuse the governments of Sulaymania and Erbil. They must govern jointly within the context of present conditions in Iraq, including the government in Baghdad, the future constitution, and relations with the neighboring states. With the help of God, Talabani hopes that unification will become a reality before the end of 2004.

With regard to the prospect of free democratic elections in Iraqi Kurdistan, it is Talabani's suggestion that these be held parallel to the general elections scheduled for January 2005. Debates on this matter will be conducted later.

In conclusion, Talabani emphasizes the demands of the Kurds once more, and underscores for all the importance of the Kurdish nation. He regrets that US troops turned from celebrated liberators to disrespected occupiers. Talabani did not wish to talk about the Americans' mistakes. Enough had already been documented by the international press.

If we compare Talabani's comments with those of 58 year old Barzani, made at a press conference on June 30, 2004, we sense that the two Kurdish leaders hold very different views. Barzani declared June 28, 2004 to be a historic day in Iraqi history, and points out the differences between the Arab and Kurdish nations. He defends the Kurdish right to autonomy, and vehemently declares that if this is not achieved an independent Kurdish state, separate from Iraq, will be needed. The least that will satisfy the Kurds is democracy and federalism. Without federalism, declares Barzani, Iraq will not remain united.

Like Talabani, Barzani believes that the occupiers are mainly responsible for the unstable conditions and the overall deplorable state of things. He believes that no security policy will be feasible unless the Iraqis are included. The population of Iraq has severely lost trust in the security forces. Barzani concludes by stressing vigorously that the Kurds will never again accept the humiliation of being considered second-class citizens.

After a thorough analysis of the two interviews, I confronted Dr. Rawenduzy with the atrocities at the Abu Ghraib prison, and the stand on the issues of the Arab television stations al-Jazeera and al-Arabia. Did these television stations apply a double standard in their reporting? After all, is not brutal torture quite normal in Arab countries?

According to information obtained directly from Baghdad, after the downfall of Saddam and his regime, freedom of the press was instituted in Iraq. Several daily, weekly, and monthly newspapers began to try their luck on the free market. Among these newspapers was al-Ahali, the liberal Kurdish weekly. The newspaper's publishers moved their offices from Kurdistan to Baghdad. What they found in Baghdad disillusioned them. They quickly grasped that this new freedom meant that newspapers did indeed exist, as did television and radio stations, but that they were paid for by the occupiers and the occupiers' partners. In other words, financing was handled by the state, just as in the "good old days". To express it boorishly, it was Berlusconi goes to Iraq.

The USA subsidized those newspapers that were of service to USA, and liberal democratic initiatives were throttled. Professional ethics went down the drain. In general, media caters to the financial backer, not to the reader. As a result, political parties exert enormous influence, reporting is not up to standard, and we find that propaganda, tirades of hatred, and glorification of violence tend to triumph over true reporting.

Although there are already two hundred newspapers of different kinds in Iraq, one cannot call these "means of communication" progressive. Such newspapers lack standards and tend to produce trash. This in turn hurts the democratic cause and assists the terrorists and fundamentalists.

In the midst of this morass, a bomb exploded – Abu Ghraib. It had been proven that several Iraqi journalists had known of torture at Abu Ghraib for some months and had been trying to obtain information from the US Army, but had been unsuccessful.

On second thoughts fundamentalists could take advantage of such reports. Now that the full truth of the depressing incidents had come to light such coverage could turn into an insidious trap seriously hampering democratic development in Iraq: people could switch to "unique and perfect" Islam again if such atrocities symbolized democracy and its effects. Al-Jazeera and al-Arabia base their commentaries on Islam.

They glorify violence, stir up hatred and intentionally remain silent on Arab barbarity.

An incident should shed light on the relationship of the press to money in this country, a relationship that includes a good deal of hypocrisy. Even as of decades ago, severe torture and mass executions had already taken place in Iraq. The victims had been the Kurds. Once Rawenduzy visited the offices of one newspaper editor after another, displaying extensive evidence that the atrocities had taken place. Aside from a few journalists, the newspapers demonstrated absolutely no interest. The editors-in-chief regretted the circumstances, but categorically refused to use their publications to take a stand on this obvious genocide. Dr. Rawenduzy was told off the record that such reports would not serve the economic interests of the country. Highly disappointed, in 1982 Rawenduzy decided to donate his entire collection of documents and photos to the Austrian National Library. It took six years to sort and record the material, and the collection was finally opened to the public in 1989.

Was this just Austrian mentality? Perhaps. In what way? Was it an example of, "All's well that ends well?" No comment.

As a trained philosopher and student of Erich Heintel, I would like to relate some of my teacher's reasoning in regard to tolerance. One may philosophically define tolerance as follows: Tolerance is a specific attitude of humanity within the scope of liberal self-determination. Humanity means humanity towards our fellow man. It is understood that humanity towards animals, often sadly neglected, should be an obligation as well. Regarding this, one can hardly speak of tolerance if one is speaking philosophically. Additionally, we must consider other aspects of tolerance, such as religious tolerance. Overall, tolerance relates specifically to our attitude towards the term "you".

If humans require specific scientific results before they take action, they will not act against science. This kind of action has nothing to do with liberal self-determination; it is merely narrow-mindedness and stupidity. In practical terms, the entire field of technical science offers no tolerance, or only a very small degree of it.

What does tolerance really mean? Tolerance circulates between technology, with a very limited margin, and something known as faith. In all of human history, the question of tolerance has been framed in this way, and it is fully justified. We also notice that fanaticism and intolerance become stronger and more terrible as liberal self-determination grows more important to humanity.

Fanaticism of belief, or doing things in the name of God, infests the entire world with the seemingly justified claim that God personally speaks through the fanatic. Heintel calls this attitude, which leads to eliminating any possible opponents, "a theocratic short circuit". In Iran Ayatollah Khomeini legalized this kind of fanaticism for himself.

Moral fanaticism in politics is equally bad. Several examples can be found in present times, and many examples if we examine more of history. With regard to politics, there is a general need to tolerate other parties' decisions. We should not condemn opposing parties, but rather should tolerate them. We should also not believe our opponents to be vicious or stupid simply because they disagree with us. If we have different opinions, we must prove them, and we must appeal to conscience and responsibility in the same way we would have our opponents appeal to us.

Therefore, party ideologies are fine and even necessary. Opposing parties are capable of reaching the same theoretical conclusions by way of completely different routes.

Unfortunately, today when we express our political opinions we all too often claim to have the only correct opinion. Consequently, we are narrow-minded and intolerant, without wishing to acknowledge that we are being narrow-minded and intolerant. A politician who thinks this way will want the absolute power to turn his ideas into a program.

According to Heintel, in a democratic constitutional state, a state with established parties, a phenomenon called "maximum motivation" will take place. Each politician is conscious that opposing politicians have justifiable motives and make justifiable decisions, even if they are different. Each politician is also aware that he can never be right 100% of the time. Such a political leader will never become a totalitarian.

Therefore, human beings should seek truth, should try to practice liberal self-determination, and should support and educate each other. Human beings are all involved in the adventure of existence. It is an adventure with a high risk, but it is unavoidable. There is no ultimate safety of a path already trodden. If we accept this, tolerance is assured and humanity attained.

Therefore, tolerance can never come from indifference, detachment, or "a frozen heart and lack of committment" (Heintel). Tolerance becomes meaningful through determination, not through incapacity, lack of influence, or hopeless skepticism. To discuss tolerance is to speak of responsibility, both in speech and in action. Otherwise, one merely engages in empty talk.

Finally, tolerance must become a joyful and decisive affirmation of reality, an affirmation that sets one free from detraction and reflections of responsibility. This affirmation of reality has most emphatically shaped the life of the Austrian exiled Kurd, Dr. Wiriya Rawenduzy, pointing him towards a life of humanitarianism and tolerance. The vicissitudes of reality have never caused him to lose his sense of humor or his patience. He possesses the ability to let things unfold naturally without losing his cool. It is this power that allows him to trust in the final order of things. His sense of humor is adverse to any narrow-minded doctrine. On life's enormous stage, despite many setbacks, Rawenduzy the human being remains strongly attached to this world, a world he embraces with unwavering humility and love.

Speaking Up for My Cause

I do not claim that my experiences with the OPEC terrorists or my present opinions on world political events are complete. I have formed my opinions because of all I have lived through, and today I put down my ideas as they exist at the moment. By no means should they be considered a compilation of historical and scientific fact.

Many confidants, both near and far, have supported me in my research, and I have made use of my own archives. Therefore, I would like to take this opportunity to thank my Kurdish friends for their invaluable assistance. I have always tried to describe the circumstances truthfully.

I herewith extend my deepest gratitude to a human being with whom I have had a strong bond of friendship for more than fifty years. It is the current president of Iraq, Mam Jalal Talabani. The roots of our friendship have been an unassailable solidarity and political teamwork, both inside and outside of Kurdistan. Although Talabani is recognized as an experienced international statesman and is in close contact with the most powerful politicians in the world, he has always kept up our friendship. Only his generous support as well as the perseverance of Bahros Galali, one of his closest associates, made the publication of the book at hand possible.

When the Iraqi Parliament democratically elected Talabani President of Iraq, it was a logical result of the Kurds' struggle for freedom and justice. Now, Talabani is placing all of his energy, political skills, and human abilities at the disposal of every Iraqi. The new Iraq should become a state of democracy and communication, a state in which all ethnic groups live together peacefully.

In June 2005, the Kurdish parliament unanimously elected Massoud Barzani President of the region of Iraqi Kurdistan. The unification of these two regions finally demonstrates the strength of the Kurds to the rest of Iraq.

So far, the government of Baghdad has not fulfilled its promises to the Kurds, and as a result the call for an independent state of Kurdistan has grown louder and louder. According to a referendum, 92% of the Kurdish population now favors independence.

The wounds the Kurdish people have sustained in the course of history have been too deep. They mistrust governments, or rather the henchmen of governments, and this mistrust is growing. Since 1962, more than 300,000 Kurds who still live in Syria have been denied Syrian citizenship. The campaigns of genocide against the Kurds live on in the Kurds' memory. The most vived memories are of Saddam Hussein's campaign of genocide, a campaign that was carried out as official state policy.

In November 2005, The Kurdish National Congress of North America (KNC) declared that *"Iraq is a failing artificial hodgepodge entity created against the desire of the Iraqi people to serve the interest of the foreign countries. The true facts are that the vast majority of Shiites want their own Islamic entity ruled under the Shari-ah Laws, Kurds want their own independent Kurdistan, and the Arab Sunnis want Iraq under their control as they had it for more than 84 years."*

KNC maintains that *"Kurdistan's independence can be achieved through peaceful struggle and processes – the era of nations achieving their independence through armed struggles and terrorist activities has passed."*

The Kurdish National Congress of North America finalizes all statements by transferring Voltaire's *"Man is free at the moment he wishes to be"* to *"Nations are free at the moment they want to be."*

With Talabani in Ankara. May 2004

In conclusion, I wish my people stability grounded in democracy. I wish them peace. And, if necessary, I wish them a state of their own. May the future quench their desire for true freedom, stability, and security; and may they one day come to understand their calling in the power play of world politics.

The flag of the Kurds has always symbolized solidarity. Its colors are red, white, and green, with a sun placed in the center. The symbol has its roots deep in the Kurdish tradition.

Red symbolizes the blood shed by the Kurdish victims.
White, together with the sun, stands for honesty and dignity.
Green represents the green of the land, and all its wild beauty.

Dr. Wiriya Rawenduzy
Vienna, Austria
February 2006

APPENDIX

The current volume was first published in German in November 2004 with the title "Der sich dem Terror stellte". Thus, the English translation is identical to the original German version with the exception of Chapter 19, which has been newly updated by Dr. Rawenduzy.

The following photos show the book launch of the German edition. Vienna, November 10, 2004.

Former Minister Erwin Lanc, at the time Minister of Transport, who provided the bus to the airport.

The presenter of the book launch Mag. Robert Wiesner (ORF) with the author of the book, Dr. Ingrid Weiss and Dr. Rawenduzy.

Discussion at the book launch (right to left): Amir Amirani (BBC London), Marlene Campell-Krammer, Dipl. Ing. Bahros Galali (diplomatic representative of the Kurds in Ankara).

Dipl. Ing. Bahros Galali congratulates the author.

Dr. Rawenduzy, Hans-Peter Slatin (Chief Physician of the Red Cross), former Minister Erwin Lanc

Dr. Rawenduzy, Univ. Prof. Dr. Alfred Giesel

Dipl. Ing. Fatima Khanaka congratulates Dr. Ingrid Weiss in the name of her Kurdish friends in Vienna.

After the book launch of the German edition journalists showed great interest in the book: newspapers, radio and TV-stations reported about the OPEC attack which took place in Vienna, the threats of terrorism today, and the situation of the Kurds in Iraq.

May 9, 2005: Interview with Vera Russwurm, Vienna ORF 2

June 17, 2005, in the morning: Live-Interview with Mrs. Nahid Ahmedi – Kurdish me-TV-Mesopotamia, Düsseldorf

June 17, 2005, afternoon: Live-Interview with Mr. Hasan Ghazi, ROJ-TV, Brussel

January 22, 2006
PUK Chief Mam Jalal Talabani and KDP Chief Massoud Barzani:
Unification of both Kurdish administrations

Copyright Photos:

All photos are from the private collection of Dr. Rawenduzy, with the exception of:

p. 84 (top) and front cover (bottom): © Gerald Zugmann,
1050 Vienna, Vogelsanggasse 32

p. 84 (bottom) and front cover (top): © Richard Röder,
1100 Vienna, Sonnwendgasse 38/14

p. 98: © Der Spiegel, Nr. 33/1976

p. 112 (bottom) and back cover: © Ernst Kainersorfer,
1040 Vienna, Fleischmanngasse 7/14

p. 120 and 121 (top): Press Agency "Hanni",
1200 Vienna, Tietzestrasse 2/16/3

p. 121 (bottom): Fritz Kern,
1050 Vienna, Schönbrunnerstrasse, 47